T0375178

THERE ARE NO BAD KIDS

By: Chuck Slate

Table of Contents – There Are No Bad Kids

Trafford rev. 04/11/2019

www.trafford.com
North America & international
toll-free: 1 888 232 4444 (USA & Canada)
fax: 812 355 4082

THERE ARE NO BAD KIDS
(Just Bad Parents)

Preface

This book was written from the heart of a foster father. That foster father would desperately hope that the United States society can return to the realization that a loving family is the most important ingredient in the raising of any child. I may, from time to time in this treatise, get off on a political tack. That is unavoidable when working in the foster care system because it is a government controlled program and as such, is political, regulative and bureaucratic. Since that is true, it is almost impossible to discuss foster care and leave politics completely out of it. The difference between a clinical approach to raising children and the real world is like night and day. I find that raising a foster child is approximate to raising my own birth children. True, foster children have been through a great deal that my children never had to go through but kids tend to be kids. If I had my way, **as a foster parent, it would give me a great deal of satisfaction if it were possible to work myself out of a job!**

> The foster care system is political, regulative and bureaucratic

I originally published this book in 1999. Things have changed so drastically in America's society and with our own lives, that I realized during this past year that I needed to publish an updated version. Most of the original book remains in tact. The changes are basically just making the dates and events current and cleaning up some punctuation. First of all, my wife and I have moved to North Carolina from Virginia and have retired from everything we were involved with in foster care. I am now 79 and Marilyn is 74. We felt that we had done our part in raising four birth children and taking 60 foster care placements. We decided it was time to retire and live out the rest of our lives in something resembling sedate living. We have done a great deal of traveling and are enjoying our remaining life. That does NOT mean that the thoughts provided in this book have become obsolete. They may even be more meaningful in today's society!

1

Chapter 1 -- The Convoluted Concept

Child Raising Concepts

We, in this country, have completely lost the following concepts:

Raising Children While Living In the Family Environment

Hillary Clinton once stated (and published a book) that it takes a village to raise a child. Ms. Clinton forgot to mention a most important aspect of that phrase. She either forgot or could not recognize that the sentence should have had a phrase added to it.

> It does **NOT** take a village to raise a child.

The phrase should state: "It takes a village to raise a child in Africa (which is where she got the idea)."

It would be nice if this country could return to a society where it takes a village to raise a child. In today's society in America it takes two strong parents to not only raise the child but try their best to protect him/her FROM the village. Those two people are a loving and caring mother and father who are dedicated to the proper raising of the next generation.

— and —

One Parent Remains in the Home

The country has, somehow, gotten off the track as far as raising children is concerned. There obviously are cases where both parents must work in order to provide adequate financial care of the children but in a very high percentage of the cases that, in my judgment, is not true!

> Is it really necessary for both parents to work?

Both parents work for a variety of reasons that have nothing to do with the absolute need of two incomes. They are in the work place to satisfy their own emotional needs, to purchase huge expensive ornate houses, more expensive cars than the family needs, big screen TVs and other 'stuff' designed to 'keep up with the Jones' and to buy drugs.

Family Time

Families who sit down to meals together have developed a rapport between the children and the parents that allows for a free and eagerly anticipated

> Real families eat together.

communication. I think spending a leisurely time at the supper table is tantamount to the bonding a child gets suckling at his mother's breast.

The continual bonding of the family on a daily basis keeps families together. It aids in the free communication of ideas and discussions of what each member of the family is doing, what interests them the most, planning family outings, family meetings and just plain family fun. Society has become so complex and each member of the family so busy with their own activities that communication and caring have become lost. The parents just want to get on with their activities and hope that the kids allow them to take part in 'adult' activities without interference from the children.

> The kids are part of the family, too.

The bottom line is: How important are our children in the priority of life? When I was a youngster, the whole family revolved around the children. That has changed! Many of the children of today are what we in foster care refer to as 'throw away' children. We are not preparing our children to be upstanding citizens prepared to take on the responsibility of keeping our country free and great. We adults are concerned with our own selfish motivations and priorities. The children, at a very early age, are left to fend for themselves. They have been referred to as 'latch key' kids. That means they raise themselves or are raised by their peers or their siblings, neither group is capable of raising themselves. How can we expect them to raise other kids? Talk about the blind leading the blind! Does anyone with a real sense of logic believe that kids can raise themselves?

> What priority do the kids have in your life?

A New Trend Has Developed

The lack of parental supervision has created a new trend in the life of teenagers. Since the parents purchase cars for those children old enough to drive (that age is far too early in my judgment) the kids have now severed the 'rope' of control and more and more of them, at the high school age, are killing themselves (and others) when leaving alcohol and drug parties. I seem to have lost count but I believe that a high school near us has had six teens killed and several hurt in a year's time.

Chapter 2 -- Where Do Foster Children Come From?

Foster children are the result of the society we just discussed. When I said that it takes only two loving parents to raise a child, there was a large assumption inherent in that statement. The assumption, of course, is that two loving parents exist in a kid's life. Given today's society a high percentage of children do not have that luxury. The foster children are generated by our society's motives. I have, many times, been asked the following question by foster children, "If my mother didn't want me, why did she have me?" The reason most foster children put it that way is because the father is not, nor has ever been, in the picture.

> Why does my mother not want me?

The only parent the child knows is their mother. I use the word mother only in the sense that this woman carried and bore the child. Generally, she is in no sense a mother. In the U.S. society today, it has become more and more the case where the father is not necessary. Why is that? The basic reason is that (as in many other instances in our society), the Government has taken the place of the father. The woman no longer needs the father's income because the Government provides that. Can the government offer love, caring, nurturing, guidance and all the other things a kid requires? Obviously not, so it (the government) ought to stay out of the picture. Back to the question!

> The Government has taken the place of the father.

When the foster child asks that question, he/she is really asking a great many questions in one. The children are lacking a family relationship that involves two parents and the children. Never having had that relationship, they are really asking, "How come you have a home with two parents who seem to love each other, who seem to work together, who seem to respect each other, who seem to love their children and who seem to love me? What happened to ME having all that?" How does a foster parent relate to that and to answer the question in a rational, unemotional way?

> Why don't I have that?

We have found that it is essential to relate to the child as though the birth mother (and Dad, in the rare case where there is a dad in the picture) is not at fault. Generally the dad is a step-father (who in a high percentage of the cases is abusive). The foster children have only one family member tie, the mother. To destroy that one remaining thread cuts the only thing the kid may have. We talk in terms of, "It wasn't your Mom's fault. She did her best. She gave you up because she felt it was the best thing for you. She did not feel she could give you what you needed to get along in the world and grow up to be a credit to society." We frequently feel the exact opposite but it gains nothing to castigate the child's birth parents. The object is to get the kids on your side so you can help them; not alienate them by denigrating their birth parents. Most kids, given time, may recognize on their own what their birth parents are really like.

> Sometimes a small lie is beneficial to protect the kid.

Chapter 3 -- Where Do We Go From Here?

Since society has allowed the moral and ethical thinking of the country to deteriorate to what we experience today, what do we do now? It is obvious that we cannot return the country to its once strong ethical and moral fiber overnight. It took more than 50 years to get to where we are. We cannot expect to turn it around overnight. My question is, "When are we going to start trying?"

Since the children are our future, the best we can do for them is to take them into a good family, show them how a family must operate in order to live and hope that enough rubs off so that we 'save' a large majority of the kids. Will we be happy with our efforts? We probably will not. Will we

> Do we make an impact?

make an impact? Probably, but we may never know. Will we keep trying? You bet! We who have dedicated ourselves to foster care have no choice. It takes a hard person to see what is happening to our children and be able to turn their back and ignore the problem.

Chapter 4 -- Raising Children Clinically or In Reality

The next question is: How do we go about turning kids around? There are many 'clinical' books on the shelves. Many of these books apply to the 'average' foster child. The "AVERAGE FOSTER CHILD" DOES NOT EXIST in real life! It's sort of like the 'average' family who has 2.2 children (what does .2 of a child look like)? Even more absurd; passing a law that makes English the official language in an English speaking society! What planet are the people from who come up with these inane suggestions? A clinical approach to child care cannot, in any way, be 'real.' Common sense (which has almost completely disappeared from society, is the way children were raised before clinical psychology became the vogue) still works today.

> What does a .2 kid look like?

This book is not intended to be clinical in any sense. It is intended to relate foster care from the viewpoint of the foster parents and the children in a real way; drawing from the experience of actually taking care of foster children. My spouse Marilyn and I took in sixty foster care placements in about seven years. All but two of them were teenagers from the ages of thirteen to seventeen (most of them were fifteen and sixteen). Early in our foster care career, we took two girls ages two and four at the same time. I decided, after that placement was over, I was much too old to be able to expend as much energy as necessary to take care of children who are not old enough to take care of their own daily needs. They virtually wore me out. I could not wait to get into the sack at the end of the day and they got us up at the crack of dawn the next day. Not a good environment for retired folks!

Chapter 5 -- Outcome Management

When I was managing in business, I always refused to allow projects to begin if the person with the idea could not or did not define how the usefulness of the project was going to be measured. I really could not see spending R&D money on projects for which we could not define their worth. Practically all of the social projects started by our government never had a measurement of their worth described before they were started. We, therefore, have spent billions on projects and have no idea whether they were effective and how effective. Oh, there are a great

> Outcome Management - or measuring the result.

many 'measurements' used by our government to justify the expenditures. Generally those are for public consumption and, in my judgment, have little or no bearing on the justification or effectiveness for the expenditure.

I located an article on the internet—The Children's Aid Society of Metropolitan Toronto has a Managed Care page. It had an extensive article entitled Outcome Management: Principles, Pointers and Pitfalls, which was written by a Dr. Davis Doty. Since Dr. Doty is a PhD, the article tends to use terms and develop theorems that may be way over the head of most of us. One problem exceedingly educated people have is that they are incapable of writing or talking without showing us their 'learned' vocabulary. In spite of that, if one is able to unravel the concept, it comes down to: Measure the worth of your efforts so that changes can be made which will make the efforts in foster care more effective. It will also allow us to learn from our mistakes. It sounds just a little like the concept used in business.

Dr. Doty uses the parable of "The Seven Blind Men and the Elephant" as an example of the intention of Outcome Management. Coming upon and touching different parts of an elephant, the seven blind men had very different impressions of what an elephant is. The one who grabbed the tail felt it was like a rope. The one who felt a leg perceived the elephant to be like a tree trunk. The one who touched the trunk thought that he held a very large snake, etc., etc. Only by integrating their different perspectives and perception did they begin to understand the complexity of the elephant.

Measuring and evaluating the different approaches, complexities of the children, the different foster home environments, etc. can provide some real insights into the ever changing environment of foster care. The variables are so complex, it may appear impossible to evaluate and gather data. The complexity is certainly true, that does not make it an impossible task. It does make it difficult but not impossible. We have computers that can search through tremendous amounts of data and come to conclusions in minutes that would take us centuries without computers. The main task is not the evaluation of data, the main task is the gathering of the data and finding a central archive for it until processing can begin. Dr. Doty's article is difficult reading and has many difficult concepts because of the language. If one can wade through that, there are good suggestions on how to approach such a concept.

Parenting is the only profession in the world where there is no training. That is not true for foster parents. Not only is there a great deal of training before placements begin but the training continues for what seems forever. However, most of the training is clinical in nature and the foster parent is forced to either continue the 'experiment' or selectively use what is presented. Accept some but "throw some out with the bath water!"

> What ever happened to the concept of parents raising their own children?

I feel it is essential that we in foster care develop a data base. This would provide a tool (which can capture 'real life experience and actions taken for successful conclusions) so that we can be more effective not only in our approach to caring for foster children but to realize a larger percentage of successes. The data base should be country wide and remove the cloak of confidentiality. IT IS A SHAME THAT PARENTS CANNOT RAISE THEIR OWN CHILDREN, RATHER THAN RELYING ON THE 'VILLAGE.' Until we can return to the concept of family, we need to do something to make our efforts more effective.

Chapter 6 -- It Does Not Take A Village To Raise A Child

There obviously are people who believe: "It takes a village to raise a child." Since Hillary Clinton dragged that phrase over from her visit to Africa and wrote her book, the phrase has been picked up (and repeated at every opportunity) by the very organizations and people who should be trying to keep families together and reduce the number of foster children. That may be true in some parts of the globe but it certainly is NOT true in the United

> 'It takes a village to raise a child' sends the wrong message!

States. In my judgment, that phrase is one of the reasons why more and more children are becoming foster children. There are several reasons why continuing to use that phrase sends the wrong message:

- The fathers of the children get the message that since the 'village' is going to raise his child he can leave for greener pastures. Therefore we have a growing number of abandoned women and children.

- The mother gets the message that it is OK for her to use drugs and/or alcohol because the 'village' will raise her child.

- Both parents get the message that they can ignore their child because the 'village' will raise the child.

- The child gets the message that he/she does not have to rely on mom and dad for support, discipline and direction because the 'village' will provide those things. He/she also gets the message that society thinks it's OK for mom and dad to abandon me.

- Government agencies get the message that since the 'village' is going to raise the child they need to provide more and more tax money to support children being raised by the 'village.'

These should not be the messages sent. The messages we should be sending are the exact opposite.

People who spout the 'village' phrase go to great lengths to list all the people who are involved with children to try to convince me that 'it does take a village to raise a child.' They list people such as doctors, teachers, psychologists, psychiatrists, social workers, etc., etc. You know what! I have never once heard them say, "The child is raised by the parents." Each of the people mentioned, of course, provides support to the child but that support is generally, and should always be, at the request of the parents. In many, many cases, the people mentioned do more harm than good. Every person in the country has the support systems which we all use, that does not mean it takes a village for us to be productive. Why does a child need more than their parents who will use the support system, if they believe it is necessary? It takes two good solid parents to determine when the support system is needed and more importantly, when it IS NOT! This country is making everything too easy. It is easy to get a divorce. It is easy to file for bankruptcy It is too easy to sue someone (everyone for everything). AND it is easy to dump children on society so the village can raise them. Like many other things in life, raising a child is difficult. That does not mean we should send the message that we will make it easy (like we try to make everything else) for you as a parent by having society (the village) raise your child. More and more of the good parents who take their responsibility seriously are going to 'in home' schooling because of the terrible subjects being taught in public schools. Also, the equally terrible environment created because of the lack of discipline in the schools.

The effect (or lack thereof) of professional therapy was discussed earlier. In short, the two parents who care and take the responsibility of raising a child (and take their responsibility seriously) are the only ones who can instill ethics, honesty, manners and all the other traits essential to make an individual a positive influence on society and his/her peers. The message that needs to be sent is: *"IT TAKES TWO DEDICATED PARENTS TO PROPERLY RAISE A CHILD!"*

Chapter 8 -- How We Got Into Foster Care

The way Marilyn and I got into foster care may very well be unique. Marilyn came home from work, at a retirement home, one day with a flier that asked, "Do you have room, can set another place at the table and have love for children? If so, you can make a difference in the life of an 'at risk' child." This flier was from an organization called Volunteer Emergency Families for Children (VEFC).

VEFC is active throughout the state of Virginia. The organization is made up of families who volunteer (with no compensation). They take 'at risk' children into their homes for a period of one to twenty-one days. The children range in age from newborn to seventeen. All children are placed by an agency (Social Services or another accredited agency). The children are screened by these agencies (as best they can on an emergency basis) to be sure that they are VEFC appropriate. That means they will likely not hurt the family or themselves and they are not on drugs or alcohol. Virginia believes that they have been the only state in the union with such a unique organization (just recently it has boiled over into North Carolina).

VEFC, a unique and effective organization.

The flier that my wife received was from that organization. I had recently retired and Marilyn was due to retire within the next two years so we decided, on the spot, that we would volunteer in the VEFC organization. We also decided that we would take in teenagers. Our peers told us we were 'nuts' to take in teenagers. That was seven years and fifty (sixty now) placements earlier. Forty-seven of those placements were when we were with the VEFC organization and we took them in on a completely voluntary basis. VEFC is a terrific concept in an emergency and the organization is well structured and effective. Members of our Social Services organization kept telling us we should become long term foster parents because they were concerned about the amount of our own money we were putting into the effort. Being on a retirement income, they felt we could not continue to afford to take care of the children without some sort of compensation.

Recently, Marilyn and I have become 'long term' foster parents and receive $400 per month, per child from Social Services -- Not much to offset eating habits of our fifty first placement. He was a fifteen year old boy who, we figure, ate $100 per week of junk food alone, plus everything else he could get his hands (or mouth) on. Most teenage males are heavy eaters but this kid went way, way beyond big eater.

What's it cost to raise a kid?

He ate if there was nothing else to do (including getting up in the middle of the night for a 'snack'). The boy's 'snacks' were twice the size of my full meals.

We had looked into becoming foster parents with an independent placing agency. These agencies pay foster parents a great deal more per month (sometimes as much as three times what Social Services pays). This is done on the assumption that at least one of the parents will not be working and will spend full time taking care of the children. Since we needed something to supplement our retirement income and we were so deeply into foster care that appeared to be a win/win situation.

Chapter 9 -- Dysfunctional Family Types

There are any number of different reasons for families to be dysfunctional. As I indicated earlier, a very high percentage of foster children placements come from single mother families (if that can be called a family). More and more fathers are running away from the responsibility of their children and leaving the mother alone to raise the child or children. The question society must ask itself is:

Why do parents bear children they either do not want or cannot properly take care of? I don't think I'm capable of clinically defining the different types of dysfunctional families so instead, I will recount some of the various reasons why children are placed into foster care:

Abuse

There a number of different abusive situations, as families become more and more abusive with each other. I will limit my comments to the abuse of children. The three most prevalent

> Child abuse is the absolute in insanity!

forms of child abuse are physical, sexual and emotional or psychological.

Physical Abuse

The physical abuse frequently is detected by either the schools or doctors. The child may complain of any number of things that are annoying them. I have seen cases of horrible mutilation from cigarette burns over a good part of the body to broken bones and anything in between.

Physical abuse may sometimes take the form of over zealous spankings (switches, belts, etc.). Frequently children who have been physically abused are extremely angry because they have no way of getting back at their abuser and must live with the pain without retaliation.

That anger frequently takes either of two directions:

1. Unreasonable reactions which may take the form of hysterics

-- or --

2. 'Clamming up' completely with responses to questions which are little more than grunts.

We have found that many times the children respond rapidly when they find that even when they do something the foster parents think is wrong, they do not receive physical punishment. They do know that their actions are not appropriate and readily see why punishment measures are needed. Most of the time, it isn't more than a week or two before we see a marked improvement in their behavior. They begin to do the stupid stuff that teenagers do but their anger subsides and/or they begin to 'come out of their shell' and begin responding in more lucid ways. After another two to three weeks, they begin to show some affection toward the foster parents. At that time, the healing process can begin in earnest.

Sexual Abuse

Sexual abuse is a somewhat more sensitive problem to solve, especially with the girls, since they have been violated and humiliated and are more inclined to think that what has happened to them is normal. Many times the girls will flirt with the foster father and attempt to entice him into some sort of sexual tryst. I have found that a gentle, "That is inappropriate behavior" will tend to make the point although it may have to be made several times. It is extremely important to show these girls that the proper physical attachment is OK (a hug, a kiss on the cheek, etc.). The worst thing a foster parent can do is to completely avoid all physical contact. Have you ever tried to show a child real affection without touching them? IMPOSSIBLE! I have tried it and not only the girls but the boys will go out of their way to hug you once you have bonded with them. I have seen clinical psychologists and staff members of group homes who frowned on a girl sitting on her foster dad's lap. I relish it! The girls learn that not all men are out to hurt them sexually. They get a feeling of comfort and ease from a foster dad that they certainly have never had from their birth father. It may be a little different with me because I am old enough to be their grandfather rather than their father. Of course, care must be taken at all times to be sure that there is not even any accidental touching of the girl's body parts which would appear sexual. There is nothing wrong with hugging, lap sitting and a kiss on the cheek. As I was cruising through clip art looking for appropriate graphics for this book, I viewed thousands of pictures. I found many, many pictures showing girls and boys of various ages sitting on Mom's lap. I found NO pictures of any girl over 5 or 6 sitting on Dad's lap. **Even the clip art has to be politically correct!** By the way hugging a boy is an excellent way of showing affection and tends to help the boy release some pent up anger against men.

> How does a foster parent show love?

Emotional or Psychological Abuse

This type of abuse is the most difficult to deal with. The biggest hurdle is the fact that the kids have been lied to by adults so much that they do not or will not believe anything they are told by an adult. Also, ALL adults are not to be trusted. Since the symptoms of other abuses seem to be the same, diagnosing this one as the culprit is difficult but it has been our experience that it can be resolved (although it takes longer) by always telling the kids the truth and making sure your actions are also truthful. Then the trick that always works in every instance is LOVE! Show the kids that even though you are not their birth parents that you do love them, support them emotionally and are not afraid to get close to them.

Runaways

Children who are runaways are sometimes the most difficult to understand because there is such a myriad of reasons why a child has chosen to run away from their home. Also, consideration must be taken to understand exactly why they were not returned to their family. The first thing the foster parent must do is to understand the reasons for the placement of a runaway child. Once that is confirmed, the runaways will probably fall into one of the other categories.

Abandonment

Abandonment of children is becoming more and more common. Since single mothers are the predominant family structure of children placed into foster care, the mothers are the ones carrying the blame for giving their children to society to take

> Conception control, not birth control.

care of. Long before that, however, the father abandoned them. It is time our society began demanding birth fathers to, at least, take financial responsibility for their lust and lack of 'birth control.' I think we should also start using the phrase CONCEPTION CONTROL rather than birth control. Once a birth starts it's pretty difficult to control.

Chapter 9A -- Respite

My definition of respite is 'giving the birth parent(s) a break.' This is a new concept for me. When I was growing up, it was inconceivable that any parent would ask another parent to take their child so they could relax and get rid of some stress. We had families raising six, eight and ten children and doing it willingly. It never entered their heads that respite was necessary or even available. There never was a need for respite because both parents were in the home and mom probably did not work. The stress level was therefore at a minimum. It

> Why is respite necessary?

also was not necessary to keep up with the Jones' because the Jones' had no more than they did. Today, I suspect, there probably is a need for respite. This is especially true in the case of 'single mothers.'

I hate that term! In most cases, ***THE MOTHER IS NOT SINGLE, SHE IS ABANDONED; AS WAS HER CHILD.*** Albeit the separation may have been mutual but the mother and children are still abandoned. This is

> Absent fathers have abandoned their family.

especially true if the father does not pay child support (which is frequently).

Chapter 10 – Phases

Testing Phase

There are many pitfalls during the testing phase. Many of these linger on throughout the other phases, as well. The foster parents must be particularly vigilant about not getting into lengthy discussions concerning 'whose fault it is.' The child will invariably try to transfer the blame to the foster parent. Guilt transference is also not reserved for children. Many 'grownups' also use the guilt transference technique to avoid admitting guilt. We have some very recent events that prove that.

> Guilt transference.

I have found that their memory is excellent when it comes to remembering any little thing the foster parent did which was not to the kid's liking. They are extremely forgetful when it comes to following the rules and accepting their responsibility. Be sure to keep the conversation 'on track.' Do not let them deflect you when they say things like, "You did it too." My answer is generally something like, "At the moment, we are discussing your actions. We can discuss mine at a later time."

You will also get kids who will try to yank your chain at any opportunity. They say things to me like, "You don't understand teenagers because you are old." I generally respond by saying, "Yes, I am old but remember, I was a teenager once. I have raised four teenagers of my own and am now in the process of trying to raise you who are one of many foster children. I believe that I have developed the credentials and experience to understand what raising a teenager is all about."

> Chain yanking.

I have found that if you agree with them immediately that you are not perfect, an argument will not start because you have immediately exhausted all their ammunition. I am also extremely tired of the phrase "You would not treat me this way if I wasn't black!" I have learned to say, "That's right!" It defuses the confrontation, takes away all their ammunition and they now know that you know they are just yanking your chain.

> Defuse

It is also necessary to be on your toes about remembering things because you may slip and say something like, "That's the third time you have done that after I told you not to do so." That's a mistake because the immediate response will be, "When were the other times?" You

> Do not allow yourself to be put on the defensive.

are now immediately on the defensive (since you are probably not keeping that detailed a record). As a foster parent (or even with your own children) you cannot make your point if you are on the defensive. When I hear comments like: "I always lose!" or "You are always right!" I know I'm on solid ground. That does not mean, however, that you never admit when you are wrong. Always admit that if it turns out to be true. Also, it doesn't hurt to apologize, when necessary.

This testing phase may go on for what seems like a terribly lengthy period of time.

Settling In Phase

The settling in phase occurs after the children have finally determined the boundaries of behavior and have, for the most part, accepted the inevitable. They, then, must determine if the boundaries are at all flexible. During the testing phase, things seemed to be rather rigid but maybe there is some leeway after all. The settling in phase is what I call the re-test phase. I pretty much know what's expected and what is not but I keep coming up with different things I want to try. Since I haven't tried this one during the testing phase, I better get it out of the way, now. Once the re-testing is fairly well complete and we all feel fairly compatible with each other, this phase ends.

Re-test

Comfortable Phase

This phase is the ultimate goal phase for the foster parents. The kids are satisfied with all the boundaries, the rules of the house, what attitudes are acceptable, etc. Now the whole family can begin to act like a family who respects, loves and cares for each other. There is a great deal of hugging which goes on in this phase and generally many "I love you(s)." Hopefully, this phase will continue until the end of the placement but it is not inconceivable that the relationship may revert back and forth between this phase and any of the others. Much of the stability depends upon the intelligence and desire of the foster child. Once the child realizes that even if their behavior is not acceptable from time to time that does not mean that the foster parents think the child is bad. We have said over and over to foster children, "We do not dislike you. We dislike what you do." That is a very important concept that the children must learn. The chances are that the environment they came from did not teach them that distinction. In fact, their past environment may have taught them that they, as a human being, were bad. That's where the "low self esteem" phrase comes from. We, as adults, often are unable to

We don't dislike you; we dislike your actions.

recognize and accept the difference.

These phases almost always run into each other and they are not as specific and clear cut as I have defined them. It also is important to remember that the children are not aware of what is going on and therefore cannot distinguish the different phases. This should give you, as a foster parent, an advantage. Remember, it is in a way a game. However, if the foster parent wins, both sides win (although the child may not see it that way).

Chapter 11 -- There Are No Bad Kids

I am digressing from the main points I wanted to make. The main points are the type of children who are placed into foster care and why they are in foster care. There are many different superficial reasons why children are placed into foster care. In my experience, in ninety-nine percent of the cases the basic under-riding fault lies with the birth parent(s). We have a saying in foster care, "THERE ARE NO BAD KIDS, JUST BAD PARENTS." In a very small minority of the cases, the child has been raised in a proper home but the child is just rotten to the core. Seldom is this the case within a caring, loving and honest home with discipline. I do not want to spend a great deal of time on those cases. I do not want to be one of those people who major in minor things. The human being has a great capacity to major in minor things.

> There are no bad kids, just bad parents.

The majority of the children for whom we have been foster parents have had no direction, no supervision and no discipline. We recognized very early (after our first placement) that we needed some house rules and that we needed to go over them as soon as possible after a new placement arrived in our home. There will be a great tendency on the part of the foster parents to 'go easy' on the kids because you realize that they have not had an easy time of it up to now. That feeling must be resisted! All of the children have had no consistent rules or guidelines to pattern their actions. The biggest need is structure and discipline until they can learn to form their own boundaries and discipline themselves. They have not been trained in self discipline. It is therefore important to not only have rules and structure but to strongly enforce the rules and not let them 'off the hook.' It is necessary to constantly be attentive to and punish for rule breaking. I find it very easy to 'let it slide this time' because I get so tired of constantly reminding them of their responsibilities. It gets to be a burden but it is a burden that the foster parents must accept. It is not OK to come in ½ hour after the promised time, even once. Most of the time it will also be necessary to continually remind them of federal, state and local laws. IT IS NOT OK IF YOU DON'T GET CAUGHT!

> NEW CONCEPT
> Anything is OK if I don't get caught.

Chapter 12 -- House Rules

Most of the children will readily agree to the 'house rules' because they just want to get settled as soon as possible. Most of the time they haven't the foggiest idea what all the rules will mean and will readily agree. We generally would sit down with them and discuss every house rule. It is necessary to hear their responses to each, quell any fears and answer questions.

House Rules

The rules of our home are as follows:

HOUSE RULES for TEENAGERS LIVING AT THE SLATE RESIDENCE

REQUIRED BY THE TEENAGERS

1. No boy friends or girl friends will be allowed without permission or when the Slates are not at home. Dates must be introduced to the Slates before permission will be given.

2. No persons of the opposite sex are permitted in the bedrooms at the same time for any reason or at any time. Children of the same sex must get permission to visit another child's bedroom. Bathroom use is limited to one person at a time. This rule applies whether the children are visiting or are members of the family.

3. Prior permission is required for all outside activities including going to neighbors, visiting friends, after school activities, etc. If you are missing for more than 30 minutes without the Slates knowing where you are, you will be considered a runaway and the Police Department will be notified.

4. Prior permission must be given before riding in anyone else's vehicle.

5. School will be attended, as required by law. Any grade below C is unacceptable. A C is considered OK but you should strive for As and Bs. Homework will be completed, as required by the teachers! The Slates will assist, if necessary. You will find that the Slates will almost always support the teacher or principal when dealing with disputes between you and the school authorities. The school punishment will be mild compared to the home punishment!

6. Telephone calls will be limited to no longer than fifteen minutes each and limited to a reasonable number per day. (The Slates will define the number allowed based upon whether the privilege is being abused.) No phone calls (in or out) after 10:00 PM. NO long distance or 900 calls will be made!

7. Household chores will be assigned and completed. Chores will be assigned shortly after arrival.

8. Attendance at meals and family meetings is compulsory unless permission is obtained in advance. All food is to be eaten in dining areas unless special permission is granted.

9. No hard rock, heavy metal, rap or any music that contains profane language. No magazines, clothing or posters that contain any of the above. Questionable materials must be reviewed by the foster parents before they are allowed.

10. Stereos, walkmans, TVs, etc. must be turned off at bedtime. Any violation will result in the loss of the offending item for one week.

11. Clothing will be appropriate and acceptable to the Slates. What is and is not acceptable will be defined by the Slates and will depend to some extent on what clothing you have available in your wardrobe. We will do our best to be consistent.

12. All lights (except for one night light) must be extinguished at bedtime.

13. Bedtimes are, as follows:

Ages 10-12 - 8:30 PM

Ages 13-15 - 9:00 PM on school nights and 10:00 PM on Friday and Saturday

Ages 16 and 17 - 10:00 PM on school nights and 11:00 PM on Friday and Saturday nights.

(Later bedtimes may be allowed for special occasions. Curfews will be ½ hour earlier than bedtimes. Curfews and bedtimes may be adjusted depending upon the time of the year and behavior of the individual).

14. Your room will be kept clean and the bed made every day.

15. The bed sheets will be changed and washed once a week.

16. A shower or bath is required at least once every other day and every day is preferable. Brushing teeth after every meal is required.

17. There will be no drinking of alcoholic beverages, use of illegal drugs or tobacco products at any time or any place.

18. Matches, lighters or any other means of starting a fire are not permitted and should never be on your person.

19. Computers will NOT be used without permission.

20. You may watch what you want on TV, with one caveat; the Slates may ask you not to watch certain channels or shows. If asked not to watch something, you are required to follow

instructions.

21. Agitating behavior such as: scaring others (including pets) being rude, threatening, teasing, stealing and refusing to answer are not acceptable behaviors.

22. A weekly allowance will be provided. The amount of the allowance is negotiable depending upon age, amount of chores, ability to handle money, etc. How the allowance is used will also be controlled.

23. You are required to clean up your own messes and not to make any unless it's an accident. This applies to keeping your shower and bathroom and bedroom clean at all times.

23. The Slates will inspect your living area from time to time to be sure the rules are being followed.

24. The Slates require your side of mutual trust.

PROVIDED BY THE SLATES

1. Room and board.
2. Transportation, as necessary.
3. Advice and counsel whether you want it or not.
4. Weekly allowance
5. Respect for you and your space.
6. Acceptance as a member of the family.
7. You will always be told the truth without exception. "I don't know" or "I won't tell you that" are acceptable truthful responses.
8. You can always expect that we will do what we say we will do. There may be times when something we have said we would do needs to be postponed. Postponements will always come with an explanation as to why it is necessary.
9. We will provide our side of mutual trust.
10. A great deal of discipline!
11. Lots and lots of love!

Since these are house rules, obviously there may be one or more that do not apply to your home or there may be others that you feel are required. A good sentence to add might be that changes will be made, as necessary.

As was stated earlier, the main reason children are remanded to the foster care system is the fault of the parents. The reasons we have so many bad parents can be written in several books. I do not intend to discuss the reasons, but almost all stem from the deterioration of families. This is a direct result of a steadily increasing decadent society that has lost any semblance of morals or ethics. It has also lost the ability or desire to discipline children. There are also many reasons for this but the main culprit is the lack of recognition by the liberals that they have created a monster. When I was in business, we constantly asked, "What have we done wrong so that we can correct it?" The liberals just seem to charge ahead at all costs with no thought at all given to the effect their policies are having on the country. Sorry -- I got on one of my pet peeve soap boxes there for a while.

> What have I done wrong, so that I can correct it?

The children placed in foster care are fighting an up hill battle from the first day they arrive in a foster care home. The children, of course, do not realize what is happening to them and why they feel as they do. All we, as foster parents, can do is to provide the life style that will show them the other side of how to live. We can only hope that they will somehow be able to accept the new life style and succeed! If they succeed -- we have succeeded! I have told many of our foster children that the reason I am sometimes angry with them is because when they do not follow the rules I feel I have failed.

> Are we ever successful?

Chapter 13 -- Foster Child Baggage

Here is a list of some of the things with which the foster child must contend:

- **Foster Child** - Just because the child has been placed into foster care is a stigma they have to live with amongst their peers.

- **Anger** - All foster children have anger that manifests itself in one form or another. They are angry because they have been taken out of their environment that they have lived with since birth. Remember these kids think a dysfunctional family is normal.

- **Birth Parents Are Never Forgotten** - No matter how badly they were treated by their parents, they still want to return to the only environment they have ever known.

- **Thrust Into a New Environment** - They are in a position where they have to live in a new environment with people they have never known.

- **Un-Learning** - They have a great deal to 'unlearn.' Unlearning a negative direction is a great deal harder than being taught the correct direction from birth.

- **Recognition of Their Situation** - It is necessary for them to recognize what has happened to them (and admit it). This is an extremely difficult task even for adults.

- **School** - It is necessary for them to keep up their school work and understand why an education is essential. Frequently they are placed in 'Home Bound' schooling that is a real farce! It cannot be considered schooling at all, in my judgment.

- **Therapy** - It may be necessary for them to be in therapy that, in itself, carries another huge amount of baggage.

That is just a partial list of high level subjects that foster children must endure. There are a great many lower level details underlying each of these, as follows:

Foster Child

Simply the fact that a child is placed into foster care will create added tension. Their peers in school and on the streets may look down on them and make all kinds of unnecessary and nasty remarks concerning the fact that they are foster children. Being in foster care,

> The thought of being a foster child is hardly ever fun!

apparently, is still not accepted in many of the kid's circles in society even though it is becoming more and more the norm. Children can be extremely cruel and any deviation from the 'norm' (whatever that is) will cause kids to be 'picked on.' That is just one more ignominy with which a foster child has to contend. There may also be a stigma in the minds of school teachers as far as foster children are concerned (although I certainly hope not). People have to understand that a kid is not in foster care because he/she wanted it and probably whatever the reason, it was not the kid's fault. Also, every kid we have had desperately wants a permanent home with siblings and two parents (they state that over and over). They know that a foster home no matter how great it is will probably not be permanent.

Anger

Most foster children are angry and even more confused than most teenagers because they have been uprooted from their home for whatever reason and are angry at the world for making that happen. The anger can have many different faces from outright physical rage to complete shut down and anything in between. Their anger can be directed at anyone but generally it is first directed at the case worker and then at the foster parents. The children cannot understand that both of these entities are doing their best to help. That is not of prime importance in the mind of the child and probably never enters their thoughts. The first

> Anger is to be expected and is normal; however how it is handled is very important.

hurdle the foster parents have to get over is to convince the child they have no reason to fear the foster parents. The foster parents are simply surrogate parents (or grandparents in our case). Generally this hurdle can be overcome but we have cases where we have not succeeded. The foster child just had so much anger they continually acted out their anger with violent physical responses such as throwing things, beating on walls, etc. Thank goodness, we have had only one child attempt to physically attack a person but we are always aware that is possible. We have tried desperately not to ask the placing agency to remove any child from our home, for cause. We feel that does more harm than good. We did have to request removal in one case because we insisted upon a child following the rules and he violently resisted.

Birth Parents Are Never Forgotten

It has been our experience that even though the child was treated very badly, the kids always want to return home no matter how bad that might be for them. There is something about the tie to a birth parent(s) that is so strong that a child could die at the hands of their parents and still feel a strong attachment. We have had children who have been beaten by their parents, sexually molested by their parents (or some other family member), taken drugs with their parents, smoked with their parents, etc. (You can fill in the, etc.). The abuse may take any of several disgusting forms. We have had children who have been with us four or five different times who have voiced the opinion that they hate their parents and love us. Yet, these same kids have wanted to return to the horrible life they originally led at the first opportunity. It is

> What did these abusive parents do that endeared them to their children?

difficult to understand. We suspect that they do not really hate their parents; they just hate what they do. Do we make a difference in the kid's lives? We like to think that we give the kids enough direction, the ability to differentiate right from wrong and enough self discipline so that they are strong enough to resist when they return home. We also suspect that the kids return to the submissive attitude in a short time. It is really difficult to return to a terrible home environment and resist forever sliding back into what they think makes life easier. (If I do what mom tells me instead of resisting, it makes life easier.)

Thrust Into a New Environment

The child has just been removed (or thrown out) from the only environment he/she has known since birth. They are now being placed into a home that is different and they must learn the new parents and what they expect. Just learning the layout of the new home and understanding such things as: What areas are off limits, where is the food, how much can I have, when can I have it, when is bedtime and why, what's my new room like, what can I watch on TV and when can I watch it, etc.? For those of you who travel either on business or on vacation, you know that there is always a period of adjustment. For most of us who are seasoned, the period is comparatively short. Think of your first trip by yourself. Getting to the airport, flying for the first time, getting from the airport to the hotel, finding everything in the hotel, getting to your first meeting,

> Will I be accepted?

meeting people you have never seen before, etc. Now just think of a young child who may never have been away from home before. He/she is meeting new adults for the first time (social worker, foster parents, therapists, new teachers, etc.), living in a new room, perhaps being a single child when used to other siblings, meeting the family of the foster parents, and most important - - "Will I be accepted by the foster parents and their family?" The most tragic blow is leaving everything and everyone I have ever known. These things are not necessarily in the front of the children's minds but they are all things that must be endured in one way or another.

Un-Learning

This may be the most difficult thing which a foster parent must accomplish. How does one go about getting the point across that what the child has been taught from birth by the birth parent(s) is mostly the wrong approach, without further destroying the child's self confidence? Add to that the fact that most teenagers believe they are expert on any subject and you have a volatile situation - - in spades! A large consideration on how to approach this is the age and the attitude of the child. Generally, the older children have a 'chip on their shoulder.' We have found that regardless of the effect on the ego of the child,

> Un-learning is the hardest part of returning to 'normal.'

it is necessary to 'knock them down a peg or two' before any type of therapy can begin. I stated the following, to one 15 year old boy that we had: "You are one person in this household, we are among the thousands in this town, the people in this town are among the hundreds of thousands in the state, the people in the state are among the millions in the country, the people in the country are among the billions on earth, the earth is a member of our galaxy, there are millions of galaxies in the universe, therefore you, as one individual, are a very small pimple on the seat of progress. Whenever you get too big for your britches think about that! How big are your problems compared to the size of the universe?" It also means extremely strong discipline is necessary.

Chapter 14 – Punishment

We, in foster care, are taught that we cannot touch the children in discipline. We believe that is absolutely wrong but abide by it because it's the 'rule' and we have promised to follow the 'rules.' We are of the opinion, however, that spanking of children, even to the age of twelve or thirteen is an absolute requirement. It generally hurts the parents more than the kid but it gets the point across that unacceptable behavior will not be tolerated.

There have been many, many articles and books printed that state that spanking a child produces a physical abuser when the child grows up. That is pure concentrated monkey milk! It was probably generated originally by a clinical psychologist who obviously never had kids. He probably wrote a paper which caused the concept to be carried forth by other clinical psychologists. Those psychologists probably never had children, either. If they have, they are probably the worst kids in the world and will most likely wind up behind bars. I have always said, "My father taught me respect in the wood shed."

My dad did not spare the rod and yet I not only loved him, I admired him. I cannot ever remember hitting either my children or my wife except to spank my children, when necessary. None of my children appear to be spouse beaters or child abusers and they certainly have never thrown their children away. It is not a hand, or a wooden spoon to the bottom that's the problem. I have also heard that one should never spank a child when the parent is angry. Again foolishness! You are angry because the kid did what you just told him fifteen minutes ago he should not do. Of course you are angry but the punishment needs to be doled out immediately when the infraction occurs. Discipline is essential! It is necessary to create boundaries and identify what happens if rules are not followed. It is necessary to be responsible for your own actions and mentally structures why laws and control are necessary in any society. The form of the punishment or discipline must be based upon the severity of the crime - - AND - - it must be immediate; something our court system has forgotten or never knew.

> Who made up these funky rules, anyway?

We have attempted to lay out beforehand the consequences of each 'crime.' Sometimes that does not work. If the child is astute (and believe me most of the kids from dysfunctional families are because they have had to be), they will decide what punishment they can tolerate (or put priorities on their punishment). They will do the things that they want to do, which fits into their scheme of acceptable punishment. It is necessary to apply the trial and error technique to determine what will or will not work with a particular child.

We have had to change the punishments for various 'crimes' as time went on because the child became 'immune' to one type or another. We do look for something that is 'near and

> Kids get immune to certain types of punishment.

dear' that we can 'take away' as a final pressure point. We feel we have been successful in about seventy-five percent of the cases. We have run into cases where no punishment has been effective. Those are the cases where we are convinced spanking would have done the trick. By the way, psychologists will also tell you never to embarrass the kids, especially in public. We try to do so whenever we get a chance, if it is warranted. There is rationale for this - - The punishment is metered out when the violation occurs. This teaches the kids to accept and deal with embarrassment (since it will happen to them frequently during their life). The kids will act up in public assuming you cannot correct them. They need to be taught differently! Acting out becomes a habit and part of the child's makeup. That trend needs to be 'short stopped' before it becomes a habit (if it is not already).

One thing must be in the fore-front of the foster parent's mind constantly. The punishment is not being doled out because there is something wrong with the kid. It is being doled out because there is something wrong with the **actions** of the kid. We had a sixteen year old who stole a hand gun from my gun case. I kept my gun case in our bedroom. He had been told (as all the kids are) that our bedroom is 'off limits.' He took the gun because one of his 'friends' told him he needed one for protection. The police recovered the gun within twenty-four hours (thank goodness). I pressed charges and told Social Services he had to be removed from our home. He was placed in a group home. We went to visit one of our other foster kids at the 'home.' I saw him on the grounds and walked up to him and hugged him. He gave me a strange look and said, "How can you press charges against me

> Would you 'press charges' against a member of your own family if they committed a crime?

and then hug me and act as if you like me the next time you see me?" I said, "As I told you when punishing you from time to time - - I am not punishing you, I'm punishing what you do. I love you but I hate what you do." To this day, I still don't think he gets the distinction. It is a really difficult concept for teenagers to handle because they are generally self oriented as part of the normal makeup of teenagers.

That is not only a tough concept for children. Have you ever had a friend whom you liked a great deal but he/she was fouling up? You tried to tell them and they immediately took it that you didn't want to be their friend anymore? Even so, it is absolutely necessary that when one of the kids commits a crime that the foster parents report him to the police. I would do that with my birth children. That the foster kids do not understand. "You would turn in your own family? My family would never do that!" Response - - Why not? Breaking the law is breaking the law no matter who is responsible. Zero tolerance must be maintained for many actions.

Speaking of punishment - - There is one licensed clinical psychologist with a Ph.D. from the University of Chicago who believes that parents should never use discipline. His name is Thomas Gordon. Dr. Gordon's booklet is entitled "What Every Parent Should Know. " It was published in 1975 and 1987 by the National committee to Prevent Child Abuse. I do not know his family status, but I only bet on sure things, and I will bet he has never fathered a child that he is responsible to raise. He claims that discipline is power and as the child gets older, the power of the parents diminishes because the only thing left is to take away the car keys. I completely disagree with this premise!

Another wacky idea!

If the parents have been smart and doled out punishment at the appropriate times and the punishment has been appropriate, the child will have become 'trained' to be a reasonable teenager long before he/she is old enough to drive. This, of course, is not the same with foster children. Raising a foster child is like training your own child from birth even though the foster child may be a teenager. We then refer back to the Un-Learning and Therapy (discussed earlier) phases. One of the chapters in Dr. Gordon's booklet is entitled "The Terrible Dangers of Discipline." From my perspective, there are no dangers in the use of discipline but there sure are many pitfalls in NOT using discipline or punishment. Our country's city and town streets and its jails are full of the results of 'spare the rod and spoil the child.' The bible is also full of examples of the need for the discipline of children. Admittedly, Dr. Gordon's booklet is over ten years old and he may have learned enough to have changed his mind by this time. Let's hope so! The main problem with raising children by clinical psychology is that it is aimed at the small minority of parents who are abusers. By today's standards, that means that all of us will be forced to raise our children based upon the standards set for abusers. Instead of punishing the abusers and continuing on, laws are passed that

That's how bureaucracy starts!

force us all to suffer (including the kids). That's what bureaucracies do. The attitude is - - We will see that no one else ever makes that mistake again! That seems kind of a strange approach but it is how bureaucracies start.

The following is a letter to the editor in the Danbury (Connecticut) New Times by Ralph Gaspard. I have never met Ralph, but he seems to recognize the problem and states it rather succinctly:

_____

"What Has It Sown?"

"*I think it started when Madelyn Murray O'Hare complained that she didn't want any prayer in our schools.*

Then someone said you had better not read the Bible in school -- the bible that says thou shalt not kill, thou shalt not steal, and love your neighbor as yourself.

Remember Dr. Benjamin Spock, who said we shouldn't spank our children when they misbehave, because their little personalities would be warped and we might damage their self-esteem?

Then someone said that teachers and principals better not discipline our children when they misbehave. And our administrators said whoa, no one in this school better touch a student when they misbehave because we don't want any bad publicity, and we surely don't want to be sued.

Then someone said, let's let our daughters have abortions if they want, and we won't even have to tell their parents.

Then someone else said, let's let our sons and daughters all the condoms they want, so they can have all the "fun" they desire, and we won't have to tell their parents.

And then some of our top officials said that it doesn't matter what we do in private as long as we do our jobs. And we said, OK, as long as I have a job and the economy is good, it doesn't matter to me what anyone does in private, it's nobody's business.

Someone said, don't stifle your children, let them make all the choices they want. Do not give them selective options to choose from. They will learn from they mistakes.

So now we're asking ourselves why our children have no conscience, why they don't know right from wrong, and why it doesn't bother them to kill. Probably, if we think about it long and hard enough, we can figure it out. I think it has a great deal to do with "We reap what we sow."

Whoa! What a concept!"

_____

It sure would be nice if the 'hands off' approach to handling children could be reversed as rapidly as possible. I don't think it is possible for this country to continue to be able, financially or emotionally, to handle many more divorces, frivolous law suits, lack of discipline of our children and the decline of families. One would think that the American people would wake up to the fact that the policies of the past 60 years have been to the extreme detriment of the country. One would also think that the politicians, psychologists, and others involved with family values and traditions would evaluate their approach and get the message that there thinking is completely convoluted.

Chapter 15 -- Recognition of Their Situation

Many of the children are in denial and refuse to accept the reason for their situation. Depending upon the reason the child is in foster care; their denial may take different forms. If the child is in foster care because they were abused and Social Services took them out of the home, they cannot recognize the problem. Whatever happened to them, which caused Social Services action, has been normal with them probably since birth therefore it must be all right. If the child has been turned over to Social Services by their parent(s), the child cannot understand (or refuse to accept) why their parent(s) no longer want them. If a child has run away from home, they have probably run away because they have had enough of a bad situation. They refuse to believe it won't get better so they can return home.

We have had children whom we took as a respite for the parent(s). One boy, who was sixteen, was placed in our care because he had a row with his mom and they were ready to do bodily harm to each other. We kept the boy for two weeks. At the end of that time, the mom came to pick him up (she had convinced Social Services that she could now handle it). She brought with her a thank you card, a rose and a cake. She thanked us over and over. As they were leaving, they hugged and told each other how much they loved one another. I told the woman, "Raising a teenager is like a marriage, you have to work at it." Her comment was, "The marriage didn't work too well!"

> Raising a teenager is like a marriage, you have to work at it!

The Foster Child and Schooling

We do our best to become involved in the school system. We try to take part in setting up their classes, their extra curricular activities and school discipline. We have many times been complimented by the schools. They frequently tell us we take more interest in our foster kids' school activities than most birth parents. We feel that is essential for several reasons: It shows the kid that we are interested in their education, it shows the school that we can be relied upon to take action, if necessary, it shows the school and the child that we will take disciplinary action in conjunction with the school, if necessary and it relieves the burden from the case worker. The foster parent is an advocate for the foster child.

> A foster parent is an advocate for foster kids.

Many of the children have been suspended from school for various reasons. Some of them have been in 'Home Bound' schooling that, to us, is a farce. The children who are in public school are generally only in class for less than five hours per day. The home bound kids are in class for two hours per day (or less) four days a week. The instructors think nothing of cutting class short on any given day (I can only handle this kid for an hour) and are not at all embarrassed by taking time off or canceling the tutoring session at any opportunity. The Home Bound children also get out of school earlier in the summer than the public schools. Why? It would seem that the Home Bound School should be in session year round to make up for all the time they are missing. How can a Home Bound school provide as much education as the public school children when they spend so little time in school?

Finding the Time To Foster

We volunteered for a great many organizations and took part in many community activities. Kids who are not in school tended to cause us a great deal of inconvenience (as if foster kids were not inconvenient to start with). The schools (mostly because of federal restrictions) are doing a terrible job when it comes to discipline. Discipline, of course, starts at home but if the parents do not or cannot provide the necessary discipline, the schools are left with no choice. The idea that the school must get the 'bad actors' out of the classroom so the other children can learn is certainly the right approach but suspending the children from school is not! The bad actors want to be suspended because they obviously do not take an interest in learning. Making them leave the school is exactly what they want. How does that solve the problem? Suspending both kids for fighting is also not the right approach. If a child is attacked by another, he has a perfect right to defend himself and certainly should not be 'found guilty' and suspended as may be true for the attacker. Kids (especially boys) have always (and always will) get into physical fights. The human being is an animal and during the puberty years they act like it, the same as all animals. Should we punish them for being human, especially the one defending himself or herself?

> Should the attackee be punished?

What is necessary is a return to corporal punishment in the schools and to stop passing children to the next grade when they have not sustained a high enough grade to pass. Oh, I know, many of you gasped when you read that. Those of you who did must have a better idea? Of course, if the child has been expelled from school and is home continually, it really places a

> The return to corporal punishment is a must if we are to regain control of our schools!

burden on us (the foster parents) because we are a busy family and into all kinds of volunteer work for the community. Also for some reason, (we know why) many children today feel that it is up to the parents to provide entertainment. It has something to do with the culture we have developed which leans toward 'the feeling that the government is supposed to take care of us' and it permeates all of society including the kids. Add to that the high-tech automation and computerization of everything. A friend of mine told me her daughter had been given a teddy bear by her grandmother. The child looked it all over, punched it a couple of times and finally asked, "Where is the switch?" If it doesn't automatically talk to you, run on the floor by itself or flash a few lights, it isn't a toy. Even the kids have grown used to having everything done for them.

Chapter 16 – Therapy

We are torn as far as professional therapy is concerned. On the one hand, we are convinced that verbal therapy is worthwhile. As mentioned earlier, verbal therapy is the great time consumer for foster parents. We spend a great deal of time with our kids in our own brand of therapy trying to help them find out where they are, why they do things they shouldn't, how they feel, teaching morals and ethics, etc. We have also from time to time indicated to Social Services when we feel a foster child is in need of 'professional' therapy. However, we question how useful verbal therapy from a professional counselor is worth. First of all, the therapist probably only sees the child no more often than once a week. We believe verbal therapy works best immediately upon the action of the child.

> Professional therapy is generally ineffective.

The foster parent verbal therapy may take the form of correction or congratulation neither of which is very useful unless it happens immediately so that the child can make an immediate connection. We have always believed **THE LIFE OF A TEENAGER IS INSTANTANEOUS!** Most teenagers cannot envision anything any farther in the future than one hour. Planning, focusing, reality, etc. are foreign to most foster children, especially boys. The girls seem to be able to look farther ahead and plan, however reality is a problem for them. The boys seem to respond to immediate stimulation and cannot think any farther ahead than the immediate stimulation.

> The life of a teenager is instantaneous.

For instance, a girl calls and says, "Come on over." He hangs up the phone and immediately sets off forgetting all other things such as: He is supposed to ask permission, he is supposed to let us know where he is going, he is supposed to tell us when he will be back, he has homework due tomorrow, he is supposed to work for a neighbor this afternoon, etc. When the girl snaps her fingers, life now becomes centered totally on her. It would be nice if it worked that way when studies are involved!

The other prevalent teen age tendency is to want all manner of THINGS! The latest of our charges had to have a bike right now! I can't wait! We found a bike for him about two months ago. He has ridden it four times. We bought him his own TV and a Nintendo. He played games constantly for about a week; hasn't touched it since!

We are of the belief that chemical therapy is not only of no use but frequently gets the child 'hooked.' The concept of 'hyper' children has been foisted on society by therapists. There are many teenagers who are 'hyper.' I was 'hyper' until I was forty. I never went anywhere without running. I always wanted to get things done in a hurry (and still do). I, many times, did things on the 'spur of the moment.' I hate to pop the therapist's bubble but all of that is fun and no one, including self serving therapists, has the right to take away the drive, the feeling of loving life and just the outright fun of living from any child by prescribing drugs. This country has gone drug happy. It appears it has become impossible to solve any social problem without drugs. The drug of choice has become Ritalin. That, of course, is being sold on the street by the very kids for whom the therapist prescribed it. Others were in pain if their prescription ran out. That's being hooked! That's withdrawal! Even if it isn't physical withdrawal, the kid obviously believes he has to have the stuff and that is mental dependence. We teach the kids the therapy jargon and convince them that they must be depended on drugs to function. They then believe it and even if we gave them placebos they would think they were dependent. In World War Two it was called brain washing.

We are of the opinion that drugs are prescribed for teenagers because it's easier for the teachers, the parents and the therapist to handle the problem if the kid is stupefied with drugs. Take nightmares for example. Most kids have nightmares. I have no idea why but that

Allow a kid be a kid!

seems to be a part of growing up. I had nightmares, all of my siblings had nightmares, and my grandchildren have nightmares. They outgrow it! They do not need drugs to keep them from having nightmares! Are the drugs given to help the kid or the care giver? For crying out loud - - leave the kids alone and let them grow up as kids instead of like zombies!

Chapter 17 -- What Is Affection?

Foster care frequently has any number of so called confidentiality issues. Take this example: (as a foster dad, think of what reaction you would take). You have taken a cute little well built girl of 16 into your home. She has shown no signs of anything but affection for you and your family. One evening, you are watching a wholesome family show (which is very difficult to find on TV). The foster girl comes flying across the room and plops herself on your lap, puts her arms around your neck and tells you she loves you. How do you respond? It's one of those situations that you may find yourself in with your spouse from time to time - - no

> **What is affection?**

matter what you do it's going to be wrong! Do you just sit there as a lump hoping she will eventually become tired and leave? Do you return her affection? Do you stumble around your tongue mumbling something about not being acceptable on her part? Do you get angry and tell her off? What can you do? When we are going to have a female placement, I try to read her as far as sexuality is concerned as soon as possible after she comes into our home.

To this point (after about 25 or so) girl placements, I have always returned the affection. A hug and telling the kid you love her is not only good for her, its good for you. It keeps you young and allows you to remember how much of a treat it was when your own birth daughter hugged you and showed you affection. It's natural and it

> **Let's quit the scare tactics!**

makes both of you bind more deeply as a family (which after all is one of the goals of a foster family). How in the world can you push a person away who is showing genuine affection? One word of caution, however -- try to never allow that kind of thing without a witness and be very careful with your hands in any case. Young girls may take an innocent touch as something far more sensual than you, at your age, ever intend. The point is - - - foster parents cannot and should not let the scare mongers create an environment that is neither good for the kid or the foster parents. Act as a family and forget the scare tactics.

I also really enjoyed 'horse play' with the kids. That's the way my family always acted, its part of our family life. If we really believe what we say that we want the kids to become a part of our family, then we had better act like a family. My spouse is always saying things like, "You'll break something." or "Act your age." She does the same thing when I play with my grandchildren.

Chapter 18 -- When The Placement Ends

Future Contact

People frequently ask us if we stay in touch with our foster children. The answer is "Yes and No." We make no attempt to intrude into their life after leaving our home. If they contact us by phone, in writing or in person, we always (and this is a must) respond in a positive way. We do the same thing with our birth children.

We have also found, in a minority of cases, that the rapport that was established between us is used against us. The children continue to contact us to ask for money, goods, clothes and just plain support. We do our best to support them emotionally and provide advice, if asked, but it ends at that point. We have done all sorts of things to support them, such as; appearing in court, acting as an intermediary with their school, counselor or Social Services.

There also have been times when we were able to assist the children and their birth parents or foster parents to see things more clearly. We do not recommend this latter approach unless a rapport has also previously been established with the other party. Injecting yourself between the child and the other parties can many times be not only unwise but can lead to devastating results for any of the players. It is important to remember that when a previous foster child asks to be heard that you listen. If he/she asks for advice, give it, but preface

> Advice and counsel.

with - - "Remember, the suggestions or comments I am about to make are my thoughts and may not be right since I am hearing only your side of the story." The second placement we had was a runaway from Wisconsin. She stayed with us three nights and two days until her parents could drive out to pick her up. That was over fifteen years ago. We have stayed in constant contact with her, since. She has had some rather rough times since leaving us but has managed to weather the storms and is doing really well. Even though she is living near her parents, she looks to us for advice. She never asks her parents because they are accusatory (she is now married with children of her own).

Her parents, instead of assisting her with whatever problem she has, they spend days telling her how bad she is, how she cannot make good decisions, etc. We find that she generally makes fairly good decisions. She has had a problem selecting men who will treat her right but apart from that she has been making excellent decisions the last three or four years. She received her GED and CNA and is planning to attend school to become an RN. We attended her wedding. She has married a wonderful guy. The day after we arrived back home, they knocked on our door stating, "What better place to spend our honeymoon than at your house?" They spent the first week of their honeymoon at our home.

Some of the other children will call us infrequently. For the most part, however, we seldom hear from the children after they leave us. We hear about how they are doing from Social Services or some of the other children but direct contact is extremely limited. As I said earlier, we make it a point not to intrude into their new life. They know where we are and how to contact us, if they wish. By the way, birth children should be given the same consideration.

Tearing Your Heart Out

If you do not become attached to almost every foster child, you probably should not be in foster care! Being attached is a vital part of the process. Becoming foster parents obviously means you have several meaningful traits, such as liking children, wanting to assist children, needing a feeling of 'giving back' (everyone has their own meaning of that term), a desire to teach these children what it is like to be a member of a real family, etc. You can add your own list. The essential ingredient is to care and if possible love. What does that do to you as a foster parent? It puts you in a vulnerable emotional position. You know that eventually the foster child is probably going to leave your care. You have worked very hard at whatever you needed to do to provide a loving home, advice and counsel, discipline and whatever else was necessary. You have fallen in love with another kid! No matter how hard you try to convince yourself that we expect them to leave, it is an extremely hard day when you have to let them go. There is a great deal of crying, hugging and consoling. It does not get any easier with each child. What does happen is that you are better able to handle the emotional tearing. It becomes easier to handle with the understanding that you have helped one more child to understand a productive, happy life and family. You have taught them how to better cope with life's ups and downs. There is also the added distress that comes later if you find out that one of your charges did not make it and is in jail, or worse! It is no different from the trauma we go through with our birth kids. Its part of being a family!

> Letting go is not easy but gets to be more normal as the number of placements goes up.

Foster Family Stress

How do your birth children see your folly? It probably makes some of your children and your friends think you have lost your sanity. Your family will undoubtedly think you should have involved them more in your decision beforehand. We have four birth children of our own, one daughter and three boys (including twins). All of our children have left home and are out on their own. We bring the foster children to visit and they, of course, spend time with the foster children when they come to visit us. It is difficult for some of them to understand why we, at our age, (I was seventy and Marilyn was sixty-six – at least we were that age when this book was originally written) constantly have new people that they have to meet and consider as an extension of our family. **CONDITION YOUR FAMILY TO KNOW WHAT TO EXPECT!**

> Condition your birth children beforehand!

My eldest son once told me, "Dad, you bring home these strange people who we have never met before and some of them are calling me brother. I'm not these kids brother and my sister is not their sister."

We only had one foster child do that but I think it will stay with my children the rest of their lives. I was at least partially responsible for that. I encouraged the foster child to act as if she was a member of the family on the assumption that it would help her to better understand a family; also, to help her understand bonding with siblings. It backfired! I neglected to consider the possible feelings and emotions of my birth children. One cannot 'ASSUME' how ones family will react. They must be consulted and informed in advance.

Your birth children must be conditioned ahead of time to understand that foster children (at least early in the placement) are children in crisis and will not act as the birth children would like. I think it did not help the foster child and it certainly upset some of our birth children. We made a mistake assuming that our children would understand without conditioning and we even believed that they would welcome our wanting to help these children. They do think we are doing a great thing but they need to know what is about to happen in advance to prepare them emotionally.

Of course there are many other areas of stress for foster parents. Dealing with kids who are not yours and who have not been raised with your particular code of ethics and priority definition place you and your whole family under stress. You as a foster parent have to do everything possible to keep yourself physically and mentally fit. Get as much rest as you can. Take a 20-30 minute break sometime in the afternoon each day and get at least an hour of exercise each day whether it's working in your garden, walking or working out in a gym. It gets difficult to find time to do anything except take care of kids, but surely, especially when school is in session you should be able to make time for exercise. One has to remember that the foster children are generally several years behind where they should be in preparing for life. It takes them a great deal of time to 'catch up.'

Playing mind games with teenagers can be extremely stressful unless you enjoy the mind games that the kids put you through. Teenagers, in particular, seem to enjoy the mind games. It seems that children are born with an inherent wish to and ability to lie about everything. I once said that I thought the main reason for a teenager to be alive was to see how many lies could be told in the shortest amount of time. We have had children who not only lied but created lies that had absolutely no basis in fact what-so-ever. Sometimes kids will fantasize trying to put themselves in a better frame of mind, I guess. I think fantasizing, especially for girls, is not only natural but probably good. There are times, however, when the fantasizing can be absolutely destructive not only to themselves but the foster parents. Inventing stories that cause the foster parents to be put in a position of trying to decide whether action should be taken based upon this kid's story. For instance suppose your fifteen year old foster daughter tells you she has been raped. Is she prone to invent untruths? If so, you now are in an untenable position. Should the authorities be notified only to spend time investigating a false story or should you forget it and pass it off as another of those 'stories?' We have yet to discover the rationale for that kind of behavior. The professional psychologists are less than helpful. They are just as stumped as we are. Their response almost always is: "That's a result of the way they were brought up and the things that happened to them." As the kids say, "Well Duh!" It does not take a genius to figure that out. What I want to know is why are they doing it and what is the solution?

> Mind games can be fun as well as annoying.

Abusive Foster Parents

As shocking as it may seem to all of us who are dedicated to taking care of someone else's kids, abusive foster parents do exist! We have all kinds of safeguards in place to try to be sure that abusive foster parents do not exist. Unfortunately, some do slip through the cracks or become abusive when they never have been before. We must do our best to be on the lookout for abusive foster parents and take the appropriate steps with the authorities when we can prove it. As mentioned earlier, the very children whom we are trying our best to help, people who are uneducated about foster care, and people who have heard horror stories about foster care in the 1930s will at times castigate fostering. That's just another bump in the road of being a foster parent. There are several pitfalls but the kids make it all worth the effort!

Chapter 19 -- Some Useful Tidbits

The following has some really useful information for kids:

14 Lessons Not Taught In School

Written by Charles Sykes -- Read by Paul Harvey on June 7, 1997

> Bring them back to reality!

1. Life is not fair. Get used to it!

2. The world won't care about your self-esteem as much as your school does. The world will expect you to accomplish something before you feel good about yourself.

3. You will not make forty-thousand dollars a year right out of high school and you won't be a VP with a car phone until you earn both.

4. If you think your teacher is tough, wait until you get a boss - he or she doesn't have tenure.

5. Flipping burgers is not beneath your dignity. Your grandparents had a different word for flipping burgers; they called it opportunity.

6. If you screw up it is not your parents fault, so don't whine about your mistakes, learn from them.

7. Before you were born your parents weren't as boring as they are now. They got that way cleaning your room and listening to you telling them how idealistic you are. So before you save the rain forest from the blood sucking parasites of your parents' generation, by delousing the closet in your room, remember how boring you will become from the same malady.

8. Your school may have done away with winners and losers but life hasn't. In some schools they've abolished failing grades. They'll give you as many times as you want to get the right answer. This, of course, bears not the slightest resemblance to anything in real life.

9. Life is not divided into semesters, you don't get summers off and very few employers are interested in helping you find yourself. Do that on your own time.

10. TV is not real life. In real life people actually have to leave the coffee shops and go to jobs.

11. Be nice to nerds. Chances are you will wind up working for a nerd.

12. Smoking does not make you cool, it makes you moronic. Ditto for purple hair, alcohol abuse, pierced body parts and drug usage.

13. Living fast and dying young is romantic only until you see one of your peers at room temperature.

14. Get up when you fall down. Michael Jordon has missed the basket nine thousand times. M.J. has lost three hundred games. Twenty-six times M.J. has been trusted to take the game winning shot and missed.

I would like to add one more - -

15. Teenagers go out and get a job so that you can leave those stupid parents forever while you still know everything!

M.J. says over and over and over again, "I have failed. That's what it costs to succeed." Most of the best baseball players in the world don't hit much over three hundred. They are out 2/3 of the time. They fail more often than they succeed but they keep trying. The best quarterbacks in the NFL rarely reach 50% passing completion, half the time they fail. They keep trying! GET UP WHEN YOU FALL DOWN!

I have had three different careers and have gone broke once. Those are the things that make strong individuals. Thank God for a wonderful woman or I probably could not have made it! That's another message -- most people need help from someone else at one or more times in their lives. Asking for help when it is needed is a sure sign of strength.

The following piece written by a social worker helps tell the story!

A SALUTE TO FOSTER PARENTS AND SUPPORTERS OF YOUTH IN CARE

by: Teresa Keller
Nottoway, Va. Department of Social
Services

Thank you
Teresa!

Such a thankless job you do
And no one knows what you go through
You're called at all hours, both day and night,
And asked to rearrange your life.

You may have plans for a weekend of bliss;
It's hard to remember you asked for this.
You straighten your shoulders and open your door -
Your family has increased one more time.

In walks a stranger, or two or three,
With lots of baggage, but no clothes, you see.
You hustle about and find what they need,
And wonder how this will ever succeed.

They come to you from broken homes
With broken hearts and broken bones,
Hungry and dirty, and mad as can be
That they were taken from their family.

You know very little about their past
Or if this placement will even last.
You give them love and try to teach
A better way to a child you can't reach.

But please remember, through stress and strife
The things you are doing may change a life.
Take it on faith, for you may never know
What they take with them when they go.

You are showing them a better way.
Perhaps they will thank you one of these days.
When they are grown and on their own
They'll remember the things they learned in your home.

And in this season of loving and giving
For folks like you, its a way of living.
You give all year of your home and your heart,
And do the job with few rewards.

So please remember when things get tough -
And you feel that you can't do enough -
You're already doing more than you know
By tending His children, He will bless you so!!

Chapter 20 – Summary

In summary - - Even though I, earlier, emphasized flexibility and each child is different, there are several concepts and approaches that are absolutely essential with every child (and by the way, with most adults, as well):

Every Child Is Different

That statement should be no news to anyone, therefore working with averages, general trends or any other cliché is not going to hack it. Every child must be treated to fit their particular needs. To arbitrarily lay down rules which state things like this or that can never be done or this or that should always be done is silly and counter productive. As I said, we have had many placements and I believe we have handled every one of those kids differently.

I Had a Bad Childhood

----- is used every day in court to justify breaking the law. The kids will also use it to their advantage because they hear the adults saying it. We cannot continue to accept that as being a valid excuse. Regardless of who taught the child to say that, every person no matter what their upbringing, has to accept responsibility for his/her own actions.

Stereotyping Should Be Avoided

Stay completely away from stereotyping children as LD, LDHD, hyper or whatever other clinical label can be placed upon them. First of all it lowers the self esteem of the child because they, themselves, believe it and their peers will make fun of them. It also makes the child believe that they are 'different' and therefore either should be treated special or as an excuse for misbehaving (Oh, I can't help it; it's because of my low self esteem). The kids pick up on these clinical expressions and use them to their benefit. In spite of what most therapists (and perhaps other adults) believe, teenagers are not stupid. In fact, they have told me many times that the adults are the stupid ones. Sometimes I think

> Stereotyping has become the norm in society. Don't use it against the kids!

that's true because we treat the older teens as if they are still children. They are NOT! They sometimes tell us they are 'pre-adults.' We should consider treating them more like adults and let them grow, if the child can handle it. Many foster children cannot.

Never Lie To Children

They have been lied to by adults most of their natural life. It is necessary to impress upon them that not all adults are liars. Some not only tell the truth but demand that the children also do so. The truth, lately, is not always popular -- but it is right! As I have said many times, "A liar needs a perfect memory so that he/she can remember what lie was told to what person, when and under what circumstances." There are also subjects, when told, can hurt a child. Just one for instance - - A child is up for adoption and a family thinks they might want him/her. The social worker tells the child about the family. Of course the kid is all excited and annoys the social worker about when he can go to visit. The prospective father is diagnosed with incurable cancer and the adoption process is stopped (for obvious reasons). The child is now devastated! Wouldn't it have been much better to not tell the kid until all was in place for visits to begin and the adoption work completed before telling the child?

> **Never lie to the kids!**

Always Do What You Say You Will

Most of the children have been brought up expecting that the adults will tell them one thing and do another. They make plans to take the kids somewhere and then at the last minute 'something comes up.' If you promise the children something, it should take a world crisis to keep you from doing it.

Caring

- is the last and most important absolute and applies to all children no matter what age. It is of the utmost importance to show (and tell) the child in every way you can that you care! It is also nice to say that we need to love every child. That is an admirable goal. We have had some children who we just could not bring ourselves to love. They were acutely aware that we cared about them or we would not have kept them in our home and tended them. The numbers of children we could not love are in a very small minority. Once in a while, though, we get one assigned to you that when they leave, your immediate comment is: "Boy, I'm glad that's over!"

Social Services would constantly tells us we are one of the best foster parent homes they had and they were constantly (good naturedly) arguing over which case worker could use us next. All of the placements we had except for perhaps two or three have desperately wanted to stay with us when it is time for them to move on. WE MUST HAVE BEEN DOING SOMETHING RIGHT!

Chapter 21 -- Case Studies

We have selected some of our placements to use as case studies. There are obviously many, many more. Each is different. Some are very sad, some are rather moving and some are just plain horrible but they all have one or more lessons connected with them.

CASE #1 -- RUNAWAY - A fifteen year old girl from Wisconsin persuaded a couple to take her with them when they came to Virginia. The parents called the Wisconsin police and they put out an APB that the police in Virginia received. While traveling on a major highway in Virginia they ran into some vehicle trouble. The police officer who stopped and assisted them recognized the girl from the description in the APB and brought her to the police station. The police contacted her parents who said they would leave right away to pick her up. While waiting for them to arrive, she needed a place to stay so they brought her to us at midnight. She stayed three nights and two days before her parents arrived.

This was really a sad case. The parents were (as far as we have been able to tell) a completely dysfunctional family. The girl had been repeatedly raped by her uncle and when she told her parents they not only ignored her, they acted as if that was a normal thing and said nothing to the uncle. He eventually, at the girl's insistence, was brought to trial and spent a considerable time in jail. All during his jail sentence, he kept filing papers to get out on probation. Of course, every time he did that, the girl had to come back into court to testify, which of course kept bringing the whole thing back to the front of her mind. The girl finally left home and had been living with a boy. She had gotten into drugs, alcohol and sex. The boy also physically mistreated her.

The first time we called her for dinner, after she was placed with us, her comment was, "Oh, your family eats together, ours never does." That was a dead giveaway as to the kind of family she had. She still writes to us, calls us on the phone and tries to come out to visit once a year. She has had several different physical problems that the doctors attribute to the rough sexual treatment by her uncle. The doctors told her she should not have children. She got pregnant by a live in boy friend. She was pregnant with twins.

They both died at birth. She then got married and got pregnant again. This time she gave birth to a premature 1 ½ pound boy. He had all sorts of physical problems mostly with his lungs. He is now two years old (when this was originally written – he is now 10 years old and doing very well – into all sorts of sports and getting good grades in school) and is coming along fine. She divorced the father and, of course, he is not paying child support. She is very proud and is taking care of herself and her child with no support from her family and is not 'on the dole' from the federal government. She does not even accept food stamps. We think the world of her. She has really matured and has certainly taken on a sense of responsibility. She loves to write poems and has given me permission to include her poems in this book. They are included as the **Appendix**. Some of them are really sad and will bring a tear to your eye. One can, however, read the progression toward recovery for this girl.

CASE #2 -- SEXUAL ABUSE - A thirteen year old girl was placed with us. She was a cute little thing. The first thing we noticed was that she had head lice. We immediately went to the store and shampooed her hair before we did anything else. She was very good about taking a shower every day and after we had gotten rid of the lice, she stayed clean. She had lived with her mother and grandmother. We are convinced her mother had not the foggiest idea who her father was. Her mother had been prostituting her daughter since she was nine years old. Finally the daughter told her mother she did not want to do that anymore and the mother threw her out of the house because she was no longer bringing in any income. She was also sexually molested by her uncle.

When she first came to us, the girl had some really atrocious habits. We took her to a very nice restaurant. She ordered steak. When it came, she immediately picked it up in her fingers and began tearing pieces off like a wolf. Her instruction on table manners began immediately! She not only would lie about everything but she invented stories that had absolutely no basis of fact. She came home from school one day and told us she had met her twin sister in school. We checked into it and found that she had only one sister who was a half sister and was several years younger.

She lived on the streets for a year or so living mostly with older men. She was picked up by Social Services and again placed in a foster home. She was placed with a family who called me (I was the Chair of the VEFC board at the time) and said, "Get this girl out of here; she is coming on to my husband." She also went into that house with head lice. The woman provided day care for two other children. She was forced to go to the houses of the other kids and get rid of the lice. Not a good experience for a foster mother.

When the girl came to us the second time she had been on the streets for a full year. Her mother turned her over to Social Services telling them that she could no longer handle the child. She had no idea about boys. Every boy who even looked at her, she intended to marry. When she came to us the second time she was attending a nearby church. She had met a twenty-five year old man. She believed that he was going to marry her. I suspect that he enjoyed the attention because he would ask her to go out. We allowed him to take her to the movies once. Upon their return, we told him that as far as we were concerned the relationship was going nowhere. He had better find someone his own age or he might get himself into a great deal of trouble. That did it! She would 'come on' to every boy she met. The two main problems she had were lying and boys. She would from time to time find some other devilment to get into, like the time she started a fire in the girls' room of the school. We (and the school) tried desperately to determine the reason for the various strange activities she got herself into. Between us, the school and her treatment counselor, we were all stumped. All we know is that the kind of behavior seen in her is consistent with the kind of environment in which she was raised. That did not help us to determine the cause so that we could guide her.

She was placed with us several times (remember, VEFC only allows 21 days). We continued to show her as much love as possible and show her where she was going wrong but nothing seemed to be of any assistance in eliminating or reducing the incidents. She continually (for two years) said that she wanted to stay with us and go to college. We fell deeply in love with her. She called us Mom and Dad and introduced us that way to others. She also called our birth children brother and sister (which upset some of them). When I hugged her, she purred! She had joined the Police Explorers and said when she became a police officer she would arrest her mother and put her in jail. We were convinced she would be with us at least until she was eighteen. She came home from a visit with her mother one Saturday and informed us that she wanted to go back to live with her mother. It had not occurred to us that would ever happen. We (especially me) were devastated! We suspect that occurred because the mother was jealous of the close ties we and the foster child developed. We also suspect that the mother had figured out that we had gotten the girl straightened out and she would now have an easy time. Wrong!! The foster girl and I had become very close. We spent as much time together as possible and the feeling of love seemed to be two way although she never once, verbally, told me she loved me. She did write it in a letter, once or twice when she was in a group home. I have still not completely resolved the emotions of having had to contend with that. It still enters my head every once in a while that her mother may be prostituting her with her new step father.

Just recently she came to visit for an evening (she has visited twice since she left us). We had a fifteen year old boy as a foster child. Before she was with him for a ½ hour, she had already given him a picture of herself that said, "I love you" and her phone number. Apparently she still has a problem with boys!

We have learned, since, that she has moved out of her mother's house and is spending a great deal of time with prostitutes and is involved with people who are dealers and users of drugs. Seems like a complete waste, doesn't it? There are times when returning the child to the birth parents does not work even at the insistence of the courts!

LETTER WRITTEN BEFORE LEAVING FOR GROUP HOME

Dear Chuck (Best Dad I ever had)

You've been so great to me I don't know how to repay you for what you have done for me since I've been at your house. I will never forget you as long as I live. I don't want to leave but I know I have to so I will keep in touch with you. I can't wait until I come back for keeps or visit.

The best part about going down there is to get into the right grade and a better personality and making new friends and getting a new start all over again.

You know what? I hope I forget about my past and worry about my future. Well, see you later Dad. I love you with all my heart!

Your Daughter,

We, Social Services and the group home staff felt that a contract would be appropriate, signed by the foster child and witnessed by a staff member at the group home. We had previously signed a contract with her that basically allayed her fears concerning whether we would keep her permanently. We referred to the contract several times after she came back but, in general, she pretty well followed what she had agreed to.

The contract follows:

CONTRACT SIGNED BEFORE RETURNING FROM GROUP HOME

Since Marilyn and Chuck Slate (my permanent foster parents) have signed a contract with me, I feel it only fair to sign a reciprocal contract with them. The conditions of my contract follow:

1. I will obey the curfews set by my foster parents. Any deviation in plans, after I leave the home, will be confirmed with a telephone call before hand.

2. I will always make every effort to tell the truth no matter what the subject. I recognize that there are times when a small lie is socially correct.

3. I will strive to confide my feelings to my foster parents especially in times of stress so that we can discuss the problem and come to a mutually agreeable resolution.

4. I will not ever partake of tobacco, liquor or drug products while living with my foster parents, either at home or when outside the home.

5. I will always complete my homework and studies in school and desperately strive to improve my grades. If I require assistance, I will ask my teachers or my foster parents for that help.

6. I will treat my peers and my foster parents with the respect they deserve. My foster mother, especially, deserves my respect.

7. I will do my best to improve my social skills (eating habits, ability to receive and give compliments, thank people for their kindness, etc.

8. I will do what I am told to do by my foster parents unless there is a mutual discussion in which everyone agrees to a change. I will never say NO to my foster parents when requested to do something. NO is a proper word to use, at times, when I am out with my peers, but not when I am at home.

9. My foster parents will be allowed to meet my friends before going out on social dates. This applies to both boys and girls.

10. I will be responsible for my own living quarters and my clothes. All must be kept clean and neat.

11. I will try my best to confide in my foster parents and believe that they are there to help me grow up, not to stifle my growth.

12. I will strive to reduce the number of times I go into my famous 'quiet zone.' I understand that to 'clam up' does not accomplish anything and generally makes matters worse because it tends to anger other people.

13. I will try my utmost to stop telling anyone outrageous lies which have no basis of fact.

14. I will admit my mistakes and take advice to assist me in attempting not to let it happen again.

15. I will happily perform any household or outside duties to which I am assigned.

16. I will limit my phone calls to no more than two fifteen minute call per twenty-four hour period.

17. I recognize that my foster parents have the right to amend (add or reduce) the list of items in this contract as the need arises.

I agree to the above conditions and therefore sign this document as a binding condition of remaining as a permanent foster child of Marilyn and Chuck Slate.

Signed

_____

Date

_____

Witness _____

Date _____

CASE #3 - STREET KID - During the first several days when this fifteen year old boy was with us, he was polite, well mannered and was delighted with his accommodations (he has a room and bath of his own). We showed him our house rules when he came and asked if he saw anything he wanted to discuss or wanted to change. He said, "Oh no, everything is cool, no problems with any of them." Once the 'honeymoon' period was over, the true child began to surface. He is still well mannered and polite when he is in someone else's house but in his home it's a different story. (This is not an unusual happenstance even with a birth child.) The child had raised himself (or his peers raised him) on the streets of Boston. We suspect most of his problems are because he has had no direction or discipline in his life. He knows who his father is but has never seen him. His mother never took much interest in him and is an alcoholic and a cocaine addict. She has given him up to Social Services. He says she emancipated him. The following are some of the symptoms of neglect and lack of upbringing.

He fights rules at every turn. We have strictly enforced the rules. That has caused a great deal of consternation. He disobeys without giving it a second thought. We have pulled him up short at each event and have doled out punishment (such as grounding, house arrest, etc.). He will not watch anything on TV that is not connected with violence or 'girls.' We have counseled him frequently concerning his preoccupation with violence. No effect!

He has no respect for authority. All adults are stupid. We have shown him by example over and over again where he has been wrong and we were right. He got the message very slowly and I think finally began believing that he could learn something from adults.

He has one brother who was shot in a drive by shooting and another who is in jail for life for killing someone. He, himself, was shot in the wrist.

He says he hates the police and the court system. Remember, he says he has been in jail more than once. We have tried getting him to sit in on our court watches to see what happens or to talk with the police. Absolute refusal! We finally ran into a problem that required police action: He and I were returning from lunch at a Taco Bell. As we were driving back toward home, he yelled, "Hey, there's a guy in a sleeping bag laying along side the road!" I said, "Get out of here!" He said, "Turn around." We turned around and drove back by and sure enough there was a person in a sleeping bag along the roadway at noon! We drove to the police station and walked into the lobby. One of the patrolmen I knew from patrolling with the Community Watch was going out on patrol. I asked him to follow us, which he did. I think he was as surprised as we were at the body lying along the roadway. Anyway, he took care of the problem and we drove off. The kid said, "He's a pretty nice guy!" He has since lost his condemnation of the police and seems comfortable with the fact that he actually was involved with an incident as a citizen.

He constantly tells you how tough he is and how much pain he can take. Yet he is afraid of any number of things such as: mice, needles, the dark, the quiet, war, etc. He will constantly ask, "How did I do? Didn't I do good?" We have tried to tell him that it not only is annoying but he will always get the answer he is looking for instead of the truth.

Taking him out in public is an experience. He will approach people he has never seen before and tap them on the shoulder, yell across a room at someone, ask completely irrelevant questions of anyone, etc. He can be really embarrassing. If we call him on it, he accuses us of embarrassing him. We cannot count the number of times we have had to apologize to others for him.

He is an absolute glutton! We figure it takes about $100/wk. To keep him in junk food, but he will gorge on almost anything. He goes through a case of soft drinks in about two days. If we take him to a restaurant, he always has a very large meal and then finishes it off with two deserts. It is normal for a teenage boy to eat a great deal but this kid exceeds anything we have ever seen. We think the eating is not because of hunger but more an emotional need.

He claims he cannot go to sleep before midnight and likes to stay up to see the sunrise. We have told him that going to bed at 8:00 PM and getting up at 6:00 AM would accomplish the same thing and provide a great deal more rest. He always leaves a light on all night and frequently plays rap music all night. No matter what we have tried, it has not worked.

He talks constantly. There seems to be no end to his conversation. It is impossible to watch a program on TV, if it does not contain violence because he will constantly talk loudly so you cannot hear. His table manners have improved but still have a long way to go. When he first came to us, he ate everything with his hands and never used a knife. We actually had to teach him how to use a knife or fork.

If he gets around other kids, he will go on at great length about how great the streets are, how he can lick three guys at once but five is a little too much. He delights in telling them how great it is to have no one tell you what to do. He went to church a few times but it got to the point where he stopped going. My wife would have to constantly be correcting him for foolish behavior, especially when the sermon was going on. He got thrown out of bible class for not paying attention and doing stupid things.

He is absolutely exasperating with his constant game playing. He says one thing and then immediately says, "Oh I was only kidding." Or he doesn't say he is kidding and you take him seriously. Then when you attempt to correct him he says he was only kidding. He will hide and jump out at anyone trying to scare them. He jumped out at me one day and it scared me so bad, I reacted immediately and threw a magazine.

He claims he doesn't lie or steal. His math instructor offered to take him paint ball shooting. He took a pair of Marilyn's underwater goggles and got them covered in paint. His instructor asked him where he got them. He said "Oh, they're mine." This was, of course, a lie. When he got home and Marilyn yelled at him for taking them without permission he said he had only borrowed them and he was kidding with his instructor. We counseled him strongly that taking things without permission is stealing. That message sunk in. He understands what stealing is and has never, to our knowledge, done so again.

He feels that it is not breaking the law if he doesn't get caught. That appears to be typical thinking for many kids who have come from dysfunctional families. He thinks rap music is about the only kind there is. We feel it is horrible. We cannot even call it music. He plays rap music all night. We have tried to expose him to other types of music since we like about everything except rock and rap. We even took him to see Nunsense - - boring!!

He has no idea how to act around girls his age. He has what he claims is a girl friend but if we had a girl friend that treated us the way she treats him, it would be bye-bye in a hurry. He hits on any girl he meets. One of our previous foster kids came to visit. Within a half hour he had a picture of her and her phone number (obviously it takes two to tango, so it was not all his fault).

He is somewhat of a hypochondriac. He worries about any little twinges and examines his body frequently for bumps, pimples and things that he thinks are not right. He asked for a complete physical. How many 15 year olds do you know who would ask for a complete physical including a blood test and we know he hates needles?

It is difficult to get through his head that designer clothes are very expensive and no better than cheaper brands, but "It's the style." (That's another thing I become tired of hearing.)

He is a huge martial arts aficionado and goes to karate class but cannot save a dime. We gave him a $10/wk. allowance and told him he had to pay for his Karate lessons. He has spent every penny on gum, candy and other junk food and has no money to pay for Karate lessons and keeps asking, "How am I going to pay for Karate?" Our approach is - - Too Bad!

He, recently, has begun to get odd jobs around the neighborhood to pay for his Karate tournaments. He kept begging me for money to go to all these tournaments. If I had given in, guess what? A woman up the street from us whom he worked for gave him a $10 check. He apparently felt that wasn't enough so he added a zero and the BANK CASHED IT!

We faithfully believe that he needed to be with an African-American family. We do not understand rap music (in fact we think it is atrocious and not music at all). We do not understand the necessity to watch MTV constantly (that is probably one of the worst channels for kids). We do not understand why it is necessary to watch fake violence (such as wrestling). We do not understand the constant need for titillation through violence or nearly naked women, etc.

He was suspended from school for a year for fighting. He has a problem mouth that will constantly get him into trouble. He thinks he is god's gift to women (doesn't matter the age). He thinks he is a great deal tougher than he really is and he will tell you constantly how good he is at everything. Putting all those things together will invariably create friction with peers.

I guess by now the picture should be fairly clear. After all that has been said, he desperately wants love and tries to hug us at every opportunity. He also wants a huge amount of praise as his asking, "How did I do?" indicates. He also tells us how much he loves us but in the next breath will tell us how tough we are and "This is not going to work." Yet, he tells everyone how much he enjoys staying with us. I keep telling Marilyn that we are constantly on his case about something. One would think he would hate us.

Since he gets very little sleep, we suspect he is under strain most of the time from lack of rest. He is a good kid at heart but has a great deal of trouble understanding how to interface with other people and how to gain recognition and praise. He has been doing very well in Home Bound schooling and we have congratulated him for that. We do not believe he is stretched enough in Home Bound schooling and has it really easy (which is not what he needs). He also is very polite most of the time, unless he is under stress, and has gotten compliments from us and others.

It is obvious to us that he is in desperate need of professional counseling and we suspect will be for many years. One of his biggest problems is that he constantly lies to himself. He tries to convince himself he is something different than he is and uses the normal teenage trick of guilt transference.

One evening, after telling him to be home at a particular time because both he and we had appointments, he arrived home over 1/2 hour late which made all of us late. He was arrogant and not the least sorry with no explanation. We sat him down and tried to get the point across one more time. He got angry stating that he had never had rules to follow before, grabbed a pair of scissors and raised them to attack me. I was ready to 'drop him' when Marilyn intervened. She was so afraid that I would hurt him that she called the agency to have him removed from our home. (I forgot to say – he is much bigger than I).

To end this dissertation, after all we have said in this case study, we liked him and spent a great deal of time and emotion on him to try to get him to see how to live. We think we have made some progress but it is hard for us to see progress because we are so close to him. As I told Marilyn, I think we have knocked the sharp edges off which may make it easier for the next people who get him. It is necessary to stay on him constantly to be sure he does not slip back. He is the biggest challenge we have had to date and only one of two children we have requested be taken out of our home!! This kind of thing always makes me feel I have failed!

CASE #4 -- MENTAL ABUSE - We received a sixteen year old boy from Social Services. We were told that he had never gotten into any trouble but was in foster care because his mother was completely dysfunctional. She did not want him. At one time she told him who his father was. He was allowed to visit the man because the man had been paying child support to his mother so they both assumed he was the father. The boy wanted so badly to have a father and a home that Social Services and the man agreed to a test to see if he was his father. The test proved negative. The boy had set his heart on the fact that this was his father and that he would be sent to college. He was extremely smart. He received straight As in school and was attending a Community College.

He was also a talented artist. There are still some of his pencil and pastel drawings in one of the shops downtown. One of his drawings was also used as a logo for the abused shelter in town. He also did some enhancement drawings for my newspaper column.

When he found out that the man was not his father, he was devastated. It looked to him as if all of his plans to go to college had been shattered! Social Services told him that there were scholarships available and there were government loans and special funding for foster children but that didn't seem to make any difference. He wanted a permanent family!

He left us to go to another family. One night he had gone to his girl friend's house and was returning home. He apparently was distraught over something that had happened between them. He wasn't paying attention and pulled out of a side road into the path of another car and was killed. At the funeral, his mother stood up in front of over 100 people and cried and said how she loved him and had done the best she could. I felt like standing up and saying, "I object!" What a hypocrite! She always told him he was no good, did not let him come to visit and was particularly obnoxious when it came to his welfare.

The following is a letter he typed on our computer. I suspect he just wanted to get it out of his system and did not intend to send it to anyone:

Homesickness

I have no true home, a different house with different people. I was told by the program's director, foster homes in this area are usually for kids that are into trouble of some sort who were free to do as they pleased in their parent's home. I was not one of these, so I had to fight to get out of the horror that was my home. Even with the cause of my horrible situation, my mother, I never stayed on one place for very long.

State to state, house to house, bad to worse, the same old story with a variable setting. What is a home? I certainly couldn't answer then, and can only answer with uncertainty now. I was just baggage to my mother, but I was profitable baggage. I contributed to her cash flow through my father, who I had never met. A hyphen which linked "child to support" kept me chained to the tortuous woman I had called mom.

That money never actually supported me. It just helped keep my mother afloat and made me her second pay check. A wallet's purpose is to hold money and you would not leave your wallet behind no matter how battered it was. In this case, the wallet was guaranteed to be filled at least once a month. Social Services was asking questions then, but the money was too valuable to her to stay in one place and wait for them to take me.

I didn't know what a home was really supposed to be like then, but when I finally discovered what was wrong, I escaped through the combined efforts of social Services, my grandparents, and myself. Now the emotional scars may be fading, but I have only escaped into a situation in which I am baggage once again. My present and 5th consecutive foster "house", is the home of Chuck and Marilyn. I have only been here 3 days. I can draw it but I can't call it a home. I've met my father, who I may be living with in the spring, and various other "new relatives" my mother had kept from me.

I have a feeling things may change for the better, but for now I'm just baggage, and, (as in my picture), I'm in the dark as to where I'm going. Some of the people I've been with were great, but as in my drawing, those homes always have an imaginary sign placed on them that states that they are only temporary. The sign actually stands for Volunteer Emergency Families for Children, which is a service in which my case has become involved. So I'm still homesick for the home I've never had.

Appendix -- The Musings Of An Abused Teenage Girl

By: Heather

These poems are dedicated to my best friends, Marilyn and Chuck

THE FACES OF SHAME

I feel, like a tree who has been defoliated.
A slender birch who has been stripped of her bark.
My trunk has become a dart board for the archer.
Inscribed on my spine is the word *SHAME*!

My limbs have been twisted, they hang by my side.
The sap has been drained, from my punctured veins.
My larynx is ruined.
I CANNOT SCREAM!

The birds of the air - are awed by their vision.
The deer cannot watch.
The squirrels bury their heads.
Even the rodents run from the sight.
The sun looks away, and my blackness remains!

SCHOOL

When I would come,
  I always went into *SCHOOL,*
  Scared and alone,
  Tough, I acted.
Someone made me mad,
  I reacted.
I always acted tough,
  No matter if I hurt,
  Or just had enough,
    Kids would look at me
  And think I was cool.
  I hardly ever made it to school,
    But as I said before,
  I was scared and lonely.
There was no-one there to tell me,
  You'll be okay,
    I'll help you through the day.

HIS GAME

John was his name,
  Hurting me was *HIS GAME*,
  It was a painful time for me,
I wanted to feel loved and carefree,
  Why was I bad, I feel so sad,
  I want to be good,
  Play like kids should.

INSANITY

I feel insane,
  a constant pain,
  It hurts pretty bad,
    keeps me sad,
    I can't let go,
  Its stuck in my soul,
    abuse is my pain,
  Why is it to blame
I'm not sure how to explain,
  but its driving me *INSANE*.

WHAT TO DO

WHAT TO DO
Should I stay, should I run,
  I'm hurting everyone,
   What's right, what's wrong,
     Sex this young is not much fun,
       What to do.
     A little girl like me has no clue,
   can you help, can you see,
     this is hurting me.

A LETTER TO GOD

GOD, let me disappear,
  I don't want this fear
Do you hate what I have done,
  Is that why you don't help,
  I'm not the one,
  I haven't hurt anyone.
Do you think its okay,
  For my uncle to do this every day.

WHERE WILL I GO

Its getting late,
  Can I still escape,
   WHERE WILL I GO,
  I'm anxious to know.
I want it to stop,
It happens a lot,
  I can't take it anymore,
   Please tell me where to go!

IS IT LOVE?

Sex all the time,
  Isn't it a crime,
   IS IT LOVE,
Or am I being taken advantage of,
  Do you think it will stop,
  Will it be okay,
   Will he ever pay,
   I have to live through this every day.

UNWILLING TO SACRIFICE LIFE

Sexual abuse has almost killed me,
    It's run down my body,
  If I don't do something about it,
    I will be dead,
  I wish I didn't have all this stuff,
    Stuck in my head,
  I've written it, I've talked it,
    It doesn't seem to help,
     Now what to do?
  Its eating me alive,
    Killing me inside,
I'm *NOT WILLING TO SACRIFICE* my life,
  He hardly sat in jail for any amount of time,
  That's what's killing me, I see him all the time,
He doesn't seem to care about anyone but himself,
  Not even the girl he paralyzed and put through hell.

A LETTER TO MY TEACHER

DEAR 5TH GRADE TEACHER:
    You found me day dreaming today,
Usually I work really hard,
Finish on time, read lots of books,
    Write poems that rhyme,
    And act like a very good girl.
You scolded me again,
    Because I was day dreaming,
      You didn't know that yesterday,
    My uncle forced me on the couch,
      Took my clothes off,
    He just sat in his big chair,
    Smiling a smile I didn't understand,
      I stood to get my clothes,
    But he took them away,
Then he came over and did things to me,
    That made me feel so ashamed,
Embarrassed and afraid,
    He laughed and thought it was funny,
I squirmed, cried, kicked and screamed,
    I couldn't get him off, he was too big,
Today I couldn't remember my "times eights"
    And I spent the afternoon day dreaming,
    But you didn't understand.

DANGER THREATENED

DANGER THREATENED,
I knew I had to get away,
  But there was no place I could go,
A young girl can hardly live the year alone,
  I stayed.
Instead I ran to my mind,
  I dodged between the messages of,
Mothers eyes and Grandma's sighs from heaven,
  Her message read, tell the truth,
    I love you dear,
  Don't tell the truth we cannot bear to hear,
Cowering from the dark recesses of an
    Attic in my head,
  I crept behind the broken furniture,
 Of my uncomfortable rage and fear
Dust grew on the weeks and months,
  Of my forbidden secret settled over me,
 as I choked in guilt.
Abandoned and abused,
 I sealed the doors,
   Hoping no one should know,
     But knowing I really,
     Wanted and needed help!

DREAMS OF HAPPINESS

DREAMS OF HAPPINESS,
run through my mind.
I wish they were real
a lot of the time,
I'm gonna have them,
I will some day,
No one can hurt me,
I'm on my way.

JUST FOR TODAY

I'm sitting here thinking of what I should be,
  People will always tell me what they want
To see,
    I'm gonna stay clean and live for today,
    I won't let anyone get in the way.
Clean is the way I'm gonna live,
  Do you think it will last
  Or just give.
I'm learning myself and my new ways,
  I'm staying clean, *JUST FOR TODAY!*

A LIFE OF FEAR

My feelings were held deep,
  I could hardly sleep,
I lived in a *LIFE OF FEAR*,
  I held my feelings very dear
The streets were cold,
  There was no where to go,
I met this man,
He lent me a hand,
  The world of drugs and sex was
    All I knew,
  Why did he take me,
    Why did he care,
  The drugs he gave me cured my fear,
Cocaine; it was the way to go,
  He wouldn't lie or hurt me,
  Should I trust this one,
  Who will soon desert me.

JAIL

JAIL is not the place for me,
  Sometimes I think I'm going crazy,
I sit in this cell,
  Its cold as all hell!
I feel scared and alone,
I really wish I was home,
I don't like the way I get
  Treated up here,
    People aren't nice and I feel insecure.

WATCHING FROM UNDERGROUND

I look at people and think - why can't I be,
  Then remember I'm only me,
I see kids dance and play all around,
  While I sit and *WATCH FROM UNDERGROUND*,
  I am trapped, there is no air
    I want to get out of here.

ITS A DREAM

ITS A DREAM that can go far,
close my eyes and look upon a star.
I wish a lot and wonder too,
I like to dream a fantasy
some day it might come true.
I may live, I may die
I just remember it can happen high.
I don't care, I don't know,
I'll just close my eyes and off I'll go.

ROUGH AS IT COMES

ROUGH AS IT COMES,
  There is always a way.
Don't worry, just think about today.
Things may happen, they always do.
Things go wrong but all I know is to move on.
Why I fight this, I don't know.
There's something out there for me.
It soon will show.

TRUST IS HARD

TRUST IS HARD,
  Grab onto someone and don't let go.
Don't worry, just hold on tight.
Take a chance and see it work.
Who am I to go berserk?
People aren't all bad it goes to show,
I've found someone who holds my soul.
It may work out, it may not,
    but for now its in my heart.

LOVE IS SO STRONG

LOVE IS SO STRONG,
it flows for long,
 I don't want it to come to an end.
It means so much, the feel, the touch,
 the intensity of the kiss,
 I can't stand to lose.
The love I've invested in you,
 The nights you hold me so long,
 the security I feel is so strong.
Believe me when I say,
it doesn't have to be today.

I CAN START ANEW

My past is away,
  it leaves everyday.
I CAN START ANEW,
  I'm just as good as you,
The things I have done,
I didn't mean to hurt anyone,
  I'm sorry I did,
I'm going to do better,
  have a good time
  and do whatever.

I LOVE YOU TODAY

I LOVE YOU TODAY,
   in my own unique way,
You are so special to me.
I miss you and dream of what's gonna be,
   maybe we can get close,
I know that's hoping for the most,
I know there's no trust,
   for me that's a must,
I want to be able to talk,
   not feel afraid,
      but be safe.
I guess I'll wait-n see,
   what's gonna happen between
      you and me.

I WANT YOU HERE

The thoughts that I'm thinking.
I'm not sure what to do.
They are bothering me.
I can't get a hold of you.
I really want to talk,
   its not as easy as I thought,
   the way that you care
      and listen to me.
I WANT YOU HERE to talk with me,
   you can't be, its not your fault.
I'll have to wait and take a walk.
I know you'll be here as soon as you can.
There's no need to rush,
   I'm taking my stand.

I KNOW YOU'LL COME BACK

Let there be space in our togetherness,
    there's no air.
I need to know why you're there,
    you say you can,
    you are always there,
    but you have lied.
I was so scared you'd be gone,
  but you told me not for long.
I KNOW YOU'LL COME BACK,
  will you stay.
You tell me things that are so sweet,
I have attached and become very close,
I'm scared to lose,
  we have grown.
Can I trust the way we are,
I can't stand to face
    this sorrow,
I pushed so long.
Maybe I was wrong.
   I know I want you in my life,
   I don't want to sacrifice.
You said I could come,
  you know I can't,
I guess this is it - -
   out of my hands.

SECRETS I KEEP

I am only as sick as my,
SECRETS I KEEP.
The things that I hide are very deep.
Can you know how
much it hurts,
The deep dark hole, ·
its very safe.
No one can hurt me,
   it will go away.
The way that I think is also bad
   and the secrets will surface,
   and fly right out,
   they can't stay in there,
   they'll find a way.
I don't want them,
   they need to leave,
   it will work out.
I know in my heart,
   so I'll live through the pain
   instead of falling apart.

IF THE TRUTH IS TOLD

IF THE TRUTH IS TOLD there's
nothing to remember,
the lies you tell,
    can never be forgotten,
don't you know
    its hard to keep up,
I can't lie, it messes,
    up my luck,
things will still be tough,
    but that's okay by me,
honesty or I'll go crazy.

JUDGE NO OTHER

The more one judges,
  the less one loves,
  the things you say,
    are not above,
Why do we look at one another,
  look at yourself,
JUDGE NO OTHER,
  we are all different in our own,
      special ways.
We can't help our physical being,
  its not the same.
Be unique and do what you like,
  forget what others think
    they are not very bright.

THE STAR HAS FALLEN

THE STAR HAS FALLEN,
  it finally has,
  its so great.
I caught a glance,
I love the sky
  and the stars above,
  where the beauty lies,
I hear the cries of the wind,
The night's still young,
  so much more to
      overcome.

WHEN I THINK OF YOU

WHEN I THINK OF YOU,
I wonder why,
the way I feel,
    then I sigh,
is it there,
Should I care,
    things have changed,
    are you aware
    I'm moving on.

DRIFTING APART

We are *DRIFTING APART*,
Its breaking my heart,
  we've become close.
You promised the most,
  I think of you today,
wish it would go away,
    you just popped right in and made yourself
    at home.
Now I'm alone.
Why did you do it.
Why did you care.
You always told me you'd be there.
Its not forever,
  but so it seems,
  I miss you.
You're in my dreams,
    the way I feel I did not know,
    Today I'm missing you so.
I know you'll be back,
    its hard to wait,
    talking on the phone's not the same,
    the things we did,
    the things we said.
Why do we do and say the things
    we say.
Do you know what's
    going on with us today.

THE WAY I FEEL

THE WAY I FEEL,
  is all okay.
When things get rough,
  I just have to say,
    help!
Its a vulnerable place for me to be,
I'm afraid of being hurt,
  its not the way it should be,
  I try to be good,
    do as I should,
It never seems enough,
  there's always other stuff.
I'm very strong.
Sometimes feeling I don't belong,
  but that's okay.
I live my life only for today.

LIVE THIS LIFE

Happiness I have not found,
  living is still all around,
   Its not as bad as it used to be,
    but things aren't the way they ought to be.
No one has changed but me, myself and I.
Its hard to live in a place,
  where no one understands why.
They sit there and use me without a care.
I am numb from the things that they say and do.
I LIVE THIS LIFE,
  not by choice.
The fight I give does no good,
  no one listens, no one should.
I'm just a rag doll,
  that's what they see.
I'm not as important,
  as I once thought I would be.

THE WAY WE WERE

Dreams that we shared,
  were once together.
Now that we split,
  they are shattered.
To go our separate ways,
  is what we said.
You keep coming back,
  and try to get in bed.
That part is through,
  it needs to end.
I miss *THE WAY WE WERE,*
  loving friends.
We can't grow,
  can't you see.
I don't use,
  you are a drugy,
  its not cool,
  its not fair,
When I wanted you to love me,
  you weren't there.

HOW LOVE'S SUPPOSED TO BE

I thought I once knew all about you,
  things have changed
  and so have you.
The things I said and what I meant,
  you took for granted without a sweat.
I was messed up and in a bad place.
Now I know its not the way.
We fight and argue,
  hurt each other bad,
  Did you know I was sad,
  The feelings I had were hidden deep,
  I never talked,
  I never cried,
  the way I felt,
  I kept inside.
THAT'S NOT *HOW LOVE'S SUPPOSED TO BE.*

I WILL NOT FALL

Sadness lives inside of me,
  its a growing tree
  the better it seems,
  I realize only in my dreams,
  the branches start to spread,
  the leaves start to die,
  do they care,
  no, I'm just there,
  not noticed unless to give.
My trunk is strong,
I WILL NOT FALL,
  but the inside is a burnt hole.
Words that are said,
  things that are done,
  its all a game to everyone.

NOW I CAN SEE

The way I was taught,
 is not my fault.
It hurts real bad,
Keeps me very sad,
 the things I do today,
 I'm happy to say,
 its all still there,
 but I don't sit and stare,
 too much time wasted.
My whole life was faded.
NOW I CAN SEE,
 it wasn't only me.
The things I did wrong,
 I hold very strong.
Never will I forget,
 the things I've seen,
 and time I've spent.
Its not funny,
 its not a game.
At least today there's less shame.
Its not my fault,
 I didn't do it.
Keep it real,
 and stick to it!

LOCKED UP

Drugs I turned,
  a lot I learned.
I did not feel,
  it was unreal,
  it wasn't a lot of fun,
  after awhile its a bum.
It got me nowhere,
  but *LOCKED UP*.
People disrespected,
I never rejected,
  addicted was the way,
  that's why I need to stay away.

THE MOUNTAINS

THE MOUNTAINS are high,
  way up in the sky.
Its very beautiful to me,
  I like to see,
  snow on the tips,
  rides and the whips.
I enjoy the peace,
  there's no one to hurt me,
  a cool autumn breeze,
  it feels very nice.
There's so much to do,
I'm stuck up there, just me and you.
We get along great,
  you'll always be there as my escape.

NEED HELP

Dreams have crossed,
  my life I lost.
I try so hard,
  stay on my guard.
I know what I need,
  I like to read,
  advice is okay,
  I *NEED HELP* today!

WHAT I AM

I am only *WHAT I AM*,
  the things they see.
I'm only a friend.
I think of what I used to be,
  its not a different person,
  its still me.
My thinking and reactions may have changed.
I'm not anymore special,
  its all okay,
  I don't wonder of tomorrow,
  I don't have time to sit in sorrow!

SCHOOL'S OKAY

I guess *SCHOOL'S OKAY*.
I go every day.
Its hard for me to see,
 why its helping to make something out of me.
New things,
more dreams,
 a new thing every day,
 I'm not a person who likes to stay,
 its a good and hopeful thing,
 I only hope to learn something.

SO BLUE

Things seem *SO BLUE,*
  I'm not with you.
I never thought,
  we'd be caught,
  but now that we are.
I wish upon a star,
  can I see, now to be,
  you are gone.
I wrote our song,
  thinking of you,
  I'm feeling so blue.

HELP SOME PEOPLE

I think of what it could have been,
  thoughts of hurt again.
I don't miss the way I used to live,
  I have a lot of things to give,
  good things, not negative,
  teach what I was never taught,
  it does not have to be that way,
  I can *HELP SOME PEOPLE* today.

I HAVE CHANGED

Things have not *CHANGED*,
  I HAVE.
The way that I do things is different.
  My friends are not the same,
  I won't play that game.
My activities are all okay,
  they don't hurt me in any way.

FORGIVENESS

FORGIVENESS is the way to,
   true health and happiness.
I can't afford to hold grudges.
It takes away my energy
   for healing.
You aren't important enough,
   to have that power.
I'm not gonna let you beat me again,
   its gonna change,
      I'm ahead.
I will stay strong and carry on.
   You don't know me,
      its been so long.
I will forgive but not forget.
   Today that's all I can accept.

THERE'S ONLY ONE ME

In all the world, there's no one,
   exactly like me.
I'm only me as you can see.
I can't change the way I am,
   I like it, I'm my friend,
      people can laugh, that's okay.
THERE'S ONLY ONE ME.
You may like me, you may not,
   I don't care, its not a lot.
I'm not here to please any more,
   if that's what you want,
      I'll close the door.
So take me as I am right now,
   things will be okay,
      I've been found.

BAD GIVEN LOVE

Its easier to speak love,
  than to practice it.
I know a way, but not today.
Words are easier said than done.
The three words can really hurt someone,
  yea, its said and we think its meant,
    but why do we bother,
     its the new trend,
      its being said way too much,
       taking advantage of the,
        bad given love.

I HOPE GOD CAN SEE

Life didn't promise to be wonderful,
  but it promises me a chance.
Its hard to sit around and wait.
Remember, life's not so great,
  things get better, that's what they say.
I don't know, I haven't seen it that way.
I'm being patient and,
  taking my time.
Will it ever end,
  its about time,
   its not up to me.
I HOPE GOD CAN SEE,
  maybe take some time for me.

DON'T GIVE UP BEFORE YOU START

We will not know unless we begin,
  DON'T GIVE UP BEFORE YOU START,
I want a chance,
  n-even a start.
I can make it if I try.
I can reach it no matter how high.
Nothing is impossible for me to see.
I am normal, a little crazy.
I like challenges as they come,
  some are boring,
    so I make them fun.

LOVE IS TAKEN FOR GRANTED

Love doesn't make the world go round.
Love makes the ride worth while.
Its taken for granted,
  used wrong.
Its a hard word to understand,
  it will come, even with a friend.
There's no need for sex or any other deeds.
Be careful of who says they love you,
  it may not be so sweet.
Its a great thing once you know,
  gives us a lot of time,
    and places to go.

START TO PLAY AGAIN

In every real person there's a,
  child hidden that wants to play.
Growing up to be a child,
  was bad and being an adult,
    was good.
The child in me has cried,
  for years.
The silent sorrow,
  the sobbing tears.
Its a good feeling to know I can,
  be let out and,
    START TO PLAY AGAIN.

These poems were written by the girl discussed in CASE 1. She is now 20 years old (when I first wrote the book – she is now in her 30s). She married a neer-do-well who treated her badly. She became pregnant and bore a son who weighed about a pound when born. He is now ten and is a ball of fire! She has had a number of physical problems. The constant day after day raping of her body has taken its toll. She has re-married a very nice well mannered and lovable man who seems to adore her. We attended their wedding and spent a few days with them. The man has two children born by an ex-wife. Heather has accepted his children as her own as has her husband toward her son. The wedding was conducted in a mid-western state. We arrived home two days after the wedding and the following day Heather and her new husband arrived at our door. She said, "What better place to spend a honeymoon than with the people we love best?"

The family is doing well financially and Heather has gotten a GED, taken additional courses and now has a job at a rehabilitation facility. We are still amazed about the feelings she has for us. She was only with us for three nights and two days at the time she ran away from her parents. In that short a time we developed a bond with her and she with us, apparently. She has always kept in touch with us and calls us her best friends. It is difficult to believe it is possible to assist someone to turn their life around in that short a time. Of course, we counseled her a great deal through letters, as well. As you might expect, we are proud of her and wish she and her family the best.

Additional information: Since she married her second husband, they have done very, very well! They own several pieces of real estate which they rent out and the construction business that her husband operates is also doing well. Her son has had many physical problems (as one might expect) since he was so small at birth. He is into all kinds of sports and is doing well in school. A daughter of her husband's (with his first wife) is married and has given them a very pretty little granddaughter. We really are very proud of them.

Index – There Are No Bad Kids

Index – There Are No Bad Kids

About the Author

From 1992 to 1999, Chuck and his wife Marilyn provided a home for foster children, sometimes taking in more than one at a time. At the original writing, they were caring for their 53rd and 54th foster child placements. The first 47 placements were completely volunteer and the Slates received no stipend. After two years, they became long term, therapeutic foster parents. The Slates have built an excellent reputation within the foster care system in Virginia as 'tough but fair' in dealing not only with the children but with the myriad of social workers who are associated with each child.

Chuck and Marilyn maintained an extremely busy volunteer schedule and their foster children were sometimes exposed to a number of meetings in a single day. It was a busy, busy family and hardly ever boring.

Chuck was also the Treasurer of the Virginia Foster Care Association (VFCA), a statewide Virginia organization dedicated to advocacy for the foster children and the foster parents. The organization is called Kidz-Together Everyone Achieves More (**K-TEAM** for short). One of Chuck's goals was to work with the VFCA to provide full four year scholarships to five foster children each year and to erect a camp in the Blue Ridge Mountains for foster children. This is obviously a long term goal since a great of financing will be needed. (Remember the original book was written in 1999)

Chuck would love to hear from you. He can be reached at chuckslate@hotmail.com